Turkish Coast

Front cover: bay and
Beydağları mountains, Lycia
region

Right: Temple of Trajan,
Pergamon

TOP 10 ATTRACTIONS

Antalya A beautiful, sophisticated city with a host of attractions *(page 73)*

Kaunos tombs, Dalyan A fine example of the Lycian tombs that are such a feature of this part of the Turkish Coast *(page 58)*

Patara beach One of the longest, loveliest beaches in Turkey, combined with an ancient city behind its dunes *(page 65)*

Pergamon • One of the greatest of the Hellenistic-Roman city states, home to one of the first health spas in history *(page 35)*

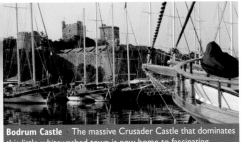

Bodrum Castle The massive Crusader Castle that dominates this little whitewashed town is now home to fascinating treasures salvaged from the deep (page 53)

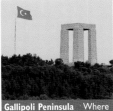

Gallipoli Peninsula Where tens of thousands of soldiers on both sides died and Atatürk made his reputation in World War I (page 27)

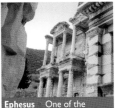

Ephesus One of the world's largest, most impressive ancient cities, instrumental in the history of early Christianity (page 45)

Ayvalik Along with its neighbour Cunda, a remarkably intact late Ottoman Greek town (page 34)

Aspendos A superbly preserved Roman theatre, venue for an annual opera and ballet festival each summer (page 79)

Pamukkale A glorious, solidified cascade of travertine pools whose hues change constantly with the light (page 51)

A PERFECT TOUR

Pick up a hire car in İstanbul, drive to Gallipoli, spending the night in Kocadere. The next day, finish touring the peninsula's World War I battlefields, crossing to Çanakkale for lunch. Drive to Troy in the early afternoon, then cross to Bozcaada for a swim and overnight. Return to the mainland, arriving at Assos for lunch and visiting the ancient acropolis. Continue to Ayvalık or Cunda for dinner and hotel. In the morning, continue to Pergamon's acropolis and Asklepion, lunching at Foça en route to Alaçatı.

Head south, via ancient Priene, Miletus and Didyma, towards Bodrum, stopping for lunch at Milas' port of Iassos. Arrive at Bodrum (or a peninsula resort) for two nights' stay. There's time for windsurfing, diving or just idling in the bazaar. Get an early start, pausing for Muğla's historic houses, en route to Datça; swim at an excellent beach to the west, with Knidos left for sunset.

After a morning swim at Altınkum, take the coastal road directly to Kuşadası, for a two-night stay there, Selçuk or Şirince village. Spend the afternoon at ancient Ephesus and the Selçuk museum. The next day drive to Pamukkale, aiming to get there for the late afternoon light.

The following day, head east to Dalyan for lunch and İztuzu beach (by car). Next morning, take a river cruise to nearby hot springs and ancient Kaunos.

DITERRANEA

SEA

OF THE TURKISH COAST

15–16   Kaş to Çıralı

Pause at ancient Myra, before swimming at Sülüklü beach and lunching at Finike. Make the trip up to Arykanda, then proceed to lodgings at Çıralı for two nights. Explore ancient Olympos, enjoy the beach and watch the Chimaera flame after dark.

17–18   Çıralı to Antalya

Leave Çıralı, stopping at Phaselis and riding the teleferik up Tahtalı Dağı, before arrival in Antalya for two nights. Spend the remaining afternoon at nearby Perge. The next day, dramatic Termessos is followed by an adrenalin-rich rafting session in the Köprülü Kanyon.

19–21   To Alanya

Proceed east, taking in the massive Aspendos theatre before a swim, lunch and ruin-spotting at Side. Stay overnight here, or continue to Alanya. Take a boat around Alanya's imposing promontory, climb to the citadel and visit the Damlataş caves. Return the car at Gazipaşa airport prior to a domestic flight back to İstanbul.

11–14   Dalyan to Kaş

Drive east for lunch at Kaya Köyü, prior to an afternoon at Tlos, Xanthos or the Letoön. Arrive at Gelemiş village, gateway to Patara, for two nights' stay. The following day sees further excursions to Saklıkent gorge or Kalkan – leaving time for Patara's magnificent beach. Continue east to Kaş for lunch, then drive to Kekova, where boatmen take you to local highlights; views from Simena's castle are dramatic towards dusk. Repeat overnight in Kaş, with a day trip to the Greek islet of Kastellórizo opposite.

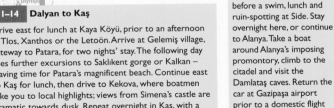

CONTENTS

91

53

38

INTRODUCTION

Statistics might tell you, for example, that Turkey grows 70 percent of the world's hazelnuts, but they don't even begin to describe the extraordinary physical beauty of soaring cliffs lapped by deep clear turquoise seas, the fresh scent of the umbrella pines in the heat of the summer sun, the shimmer of the full moon above the travertine pools at Pamukkale, the simple pleasure of eating calamari on a shady terrace beside a colourful fishing harbour, and the venerable history everywhere you look. Nevertheless, Turkey's vital statistics are mind-bogglingly huge.

Geography and Landscape

The Turkish coast (not all of it covered in this book) is a staggering 7,200km (4,474 miles) in length, comprising the shores of the Black Sea, the Bosphorus Straits (at İstanbul), the Sea of Marmara, the Dardanelles, the Aegean Sea (in the west) and the Mediterranean (in the south). Turkey connects Europe with Asia – in fact, only three percent of the country's land area is in Europe – a bridging function that has for centuries been an important element in the history of Asia Minor.

The west coast between Thrace and Marmaris is characterised by bays, peninsulas reaching out into the Aegean, many islets, and a hinterland dominated by

Left: dropping anchor on the Lycian coast

Population pattern

Two-thirds of Turkey's 73 million population live within about 30km (18 miles) of the coast, in one of four giant cities – İstanbul, İzmir, Antalya and Adana or the many towns and ribbon developments that line the roads between them. Only the capital Ankara is well inland.

broad, fertile river valleys and alluvial plains. The best scenery is to be found a little further east, along the Lycian Coast between Fethiye and Antalya, where the Toros (Taurus) Mountains swoop directly down to the sea, their feet clad in sandy coves and caves carved by the crashing surf, their jagged limestone ridges fringed by giant cedars. This region, called Lycia in antiquity, is a relatively difficult region to explore, although the construction of a coast road in the 1980s has helped to open it up. At middle altitudes, the pine forests and herbal scrub are a riot of colour and aroma in spring, while those lowland valleys not blanketed by plastic hothouses support citrus and almond groves.

The convoluted peninsulas of Bozburun and Datça, respectively south and west of Marmaris, are also alluring. There are also some very pretty areas along the north Aegean coast, while the south Aegean is generally flatter and more

On the road between Kalkan and Kaş on the Lycian Coast

built-up. The area immediately to the east of Antalya has a broad fertile coastal plain – formerly known as Pamphylia – that makes for glorious long sandy beaches but rather boring views, and you have to go 20 to 30km (12–18 miles) inland if you want mountains and canyons.

Historic Crossroads

Think of a great civilisation and chances are they will have had a foothold in Anatolia at some point – the Hittites, Persians, Greeks, Romans, Arabs, Byzantines and Ottomans, for starters.

The ruins of ancient Knidos, near Marmaris

Cleopatra owned a small chunk, given to her as a wedding present by Mark Anthony. Norman crusaders set up kingdoms in Constantinople, Antioch and Edessa. Genghis Khan, Timur and their Mongol hordes swept through, briefly and violently. Most of them left a physical legacy, part of a magnificent smorgasbord of history that spans several thousand years, many major cultures, several religions and figures such as Helen of Troy, Croesus (as in rich as…) and even Santa Claus (St Nicholas).

The Seljuk Turks after whom Atatürk chose to name his nation were in fact a small group who only arrived in Anatolia in the 11th century AD from their Central Asian homeland. Today, while the Turks are remarkably united as a nation, invasions and migrations have created an extraordinary racial mix. The differences in features can be seen, from faces straight off a Grecian urn in the northwest, to the almost Mongol fea-

tures in the blue eyes and fair complexion of nomads in the far south. About 20 percent of the country's population are Kurds; about 1 percent are Arab; 98 percent are Muslim, either Sunni or Alevî.

East Meets West

Throughout its long history, Turkey has faced two directions at once, acting as a trading route (part of the Silk Road), crossroads and political conduit between the great civilisations of Europe and the East. These days, Turkey is again pulled in two directions, between Atatürk's pro-Western, secular approach – those (not

Taking in the view in Candarli

necessarily the secularists) whose top priority is to join the EU – and those who would prefer to remain an independent regional power while preserving traditional values. The two sides contend in both lawcourts and parliament and women, whether they choose to wear headscarves for religious or political reasons, as a fashion statement, or to keep the dust off their hair, are in the front line.

Although more Turks now live in cities or large towns than out in the countryside, agriculture and village life are still prominent, with rural women in baggy trousers and cardigans, men in flat caps, herds of livestock and acres of plastic hothouses nursing the world's finest tomatoes and aubergines. But the major cities and resorts, the latter in a wafer-thin coastal fringe, have a veneer of sophistication that matches any in the world, with fine dining and clubs filled with beautiful people in designer clothes and plenty of bling. Alongside them are increasing battalions of identikit villas and apartment blocks, as Turkey's interior-dwellers claim a holiday home by the sea – a trend that accelerated in the 1980s as an anti-inflationary investment. Beautiful, unspoilt coastline tends to be protected by the military, archaeology or forestry services, and luckily there are still plenty of such stretches.

Choosing Your Spot

Which bit of coast is best for you? There is a rough division by nationality *(see below)*, but much more important is to choose by interest. There are ancient monuments almost everywhere you look, but if you want to explore the region in detail, either do a touring holiday or pick an appropriate base. Stay in around Ayvalık for visiting Pergamon and Assos; Çanakkale for Gallipoli and Troy, and the two inhabited Aegean islands; Kuşadası for Ephesus, Aphrodisias, Didyma, Priene and Miletus; the Lycian Coast for an embarrassment of riches including

The National Divide

People have joked for years about the great Anglo-German sun-lounger battle, but in Turkey they took it one stage further, dividing up the coast. The Brits traditionally dominated the Aegean and Turquoise Coast as far as Ölüdeniz and the Germans the stretch from Çıralı to Alanya. Beyond Alanya was the province of the Turks and Arabs. The Lycian Coast between was a sort of gentrified no-man's land, shared by older, wealthier tourists of various nations. These days, it's getting more confused as British house-buyers head for the south coast, the Russians arrive en masse and the Turkish middle classes scatter along the Aegean and Lycian coasts for seaside holidays.

Xanthos, the Letoön, Patara, Tlos, Olympos and Phaselis; and Antalya for Perge and Aspendos.

Socially, Bodrum and Kalkan are the most upmarket resorts, with Kaş, Dalyan and Foça close behind. Antalya, Datça and Ayvalık are middle of the road, while Kuşadası and Ölüdeniz fall at the lower end of the spectrum, although there are exceptions to all. Olympos, near Antalya, is the closest the coast has to a backpacker hangout, while Behramkale (Assos) and Bozcaada plus Gökçeada islands in the north Aegean are favourites of İstanbul's trendy set. Belek is full of fanatical golfers. However, exceptions to the generalisations abound, and anyway many foreign tourists stay within the confines of an all-inclusive resort and don't affect nearby towns.

Enjoying a resort in Ölüdeniz

If you crave a long sandy beach, head for Patara or the area between Antalya and Alanya, which also has the most gently sloping shoreline, ideal for small children. The Lycian Coast, west of Antalya, has fabulous scenery and great swimming, but few actual beaches (many of these pebbly and sharply shelving). The deeply indented coast around Bodrum and Marmaris, is perfect for watersports of all kinds, especially yachting, windsurfing and diving. The Aegean Coast is generally more family friendly, with the best beaches found north of İzmir.

A BRIEF HISTORY

Modern Turkey has had many identities across the millennia; some even claim this was the home of the Garden of Eden. The earliest humanoid bones found date back some 1 million years. But the real human history of the region starts in around 9000BC, at the time when the first hunter-gatherers were beginning to worship at temples and the first farmers were growing grain (both in southeast Turkey). By 7000BC, tent-dwellers were painting caves at Beldibi near Antalya and by 6300BC a community of around 5,000 were using irrigation and domesticating livestock at Çatalhöyük, south of Konya, officially the second-oldest town in the world (after Jericho).

The Time of Legends

Fast forward to around 2000BC when the Hittites arrived further east, creating an empire in central Anatolia that lasted for 800 years and challenged the might of Babylon and Egypt. Meanwhile, on the Aegean coast, Troy had already been flourishing for over 1,000 years and was to continue trading and scrapping with its neighbours for almost another 800 years before the epic siege, in c.1250BC, that was immortalised by Homer in *The Iliad*. The war was probably more about trade routes than abduction but whatever the cause, the Trojan campaign united the Greeks against a common enemy and introduced the first Hellenic colonists to Anatolia.

The Trojan Horse

Greek Diaspora

From the 12th century BC onwards, wave after wave of the so-called Sea Peoples moved into and across Anatolia, the Hittite empire crumbling before them. First the Phrygians from Thrace and the northwest moved into the centre of the peninsula, best known for King Midas (of the golden touch; 7th century BC). Then the Lydians settled inland from the Aegean coast, with their capital at Sardis, again famed for a stupendously rich monarch, King Croesus (r. 561–546BC), credited with the invention of dice and issuing the first gold coins for general circulation. To the south, the wild Torus mountains were settled by the Lycians, apparently an indigenous people whom the Hittites described as a proudly independent, ungovernable, matriarchal society. The gentler lands east of modern Antalya were settled by the Pamphylians, and the

Lycian Tombs

Proud inventors of the world's earliest known democratic federation (supposedly one of the models on which the constitution of the United States was based), the Lycians left surprisingly little in the way of archaeological evidence other than a large supply of extraordinarily elaborate tombs – 1,085 at last count, in many shapes and sizes. The earliest include square-cut pillar-tombs such as the Harpy Tomb at Xanthos, and there are also chunky free-standing sarcophagi with three compartments (for slaves and companions, for grave goods and for the main inhabitant) and an elaborate often Gothic lid like the keel of an upturned ship. More common are rock-cut tombs cut into a cliff face, many modelled on private houses, even copying wooden carpenters' pegs in stone, the most elaborate, in Pınara, Termessos, and Myra mimic grand temple facades, with the whole edifice painted as well as carved. The dead lay on stone benches surrounded by grave goods, the entrance blocked by sliding doors.

Termessos rock tombs

eastern Mediterranean by the Cilicians. Inland, until the 8th century BC, there was a second flowering of a smaller neo-Hittite kingdom.

Clash of the Titans

All these people were builders and traders, creating great cities along the coast, such as Ephesus, a great port and cult centre sacred to Artemis, which traded not only with each other and with Europe, but with the caravans from the east. It was a conspicuous display of wealth that inevitably drew envious eyes.

In 546BC, Cyrus II of Persia invaded, turning the region into a dependency of the Persian Empire for nearly 200 years until, in 334BC, Alexander of Macedonia (the Great) turned his greedy young eyes on Anatolia, defeating King Darius III of Persia at the epic battle of Issos in 333BC.

Anatolia became Greek again, but Alexander was better at conquering than ruling and he continued east, only to die, absurdly young, in 323BC. Anatolia was divided between four of his generals – Seleukos Nikator, Ptolemy, Antigonos and Lysimakhos. With classical Greece as an example, temples and colonnades, baths, theatres and all the other essentials of sophisticated city life were erected and decorated with magnificent statuary. Hellenistic monuments which survive today include the the temples at Didyma and Priene, and the great gates of Perge. The city-states flourished, re-asserting their independence or even forming political federations such as the powerful Lycian Federation.

Romans and Christians

Then, in 133BC, the last king of Pergamon, Attalos III, bequeathed his kingdom to Rome. Within a few years, Anatolia had become the Roman province of Asia Minor. The city states lost their independence but gained protection and pa-

The Temple of Athena at Priene

tronage; from this era date such fine monuments as the Aspendos theatre and the Library of Celsus at Ephesus. Fresh invasion attempts by the Gauls (Galatians) and Parthians were repulsed and Mediterranean piracy was cleaned up by Pompey. Mark Antony met Cleopatra in Tarsus and married her near Antioch (modern Antakya), which is also where Sts Peter, Paul and Barnabas supposedly met in a hidden cave-church and first dubbed the new religion Christianity.

Between AD40 and 55 St Paul intermittently preached Christianity across Anatolia, and despite protracted Roman repression the religion continued to spread until, in AD 311, the Edict of Galerius halted the persecution of Christians. The eastern Roman Emperor Constantine (r. 306–37) actively favoured Christianity – though it did not become the state religion until after his death – and sent his mother (St Helena) to Jerusalem on a relic hunt. In 325, he convened the Council of Nicaea (İznik) which stipulated the basic tenets of faith in the Nicene Creed.

The Byzantine Empire

Although he grew up in Diocletian's court, and secured his position at the Battle of Milvian Bridge in AD 312, Constantine was always more at home further east. In 324, with Rome under severe pressure from the barbarians, he chose the site of the eastern imperial capital after a revelatory dream and Constantinople grew from the small Greek city of Byzantium. Shortly after his death, the Roman Empire formally split in two and the Byzantine Empire began its glorious ascendancy. It was an era of Orthodox monasticism, extreme wealth and opulence, fed as ever by international trade with both east and west, and of extreme courtly intrigue. With power centralised at Constantinople, the importance of the coastal cities began to decline, their wealth declining further as many of their harbours silted up, stranding them inland.

Islam and the Iconoclasts

The opulence of the Byzantine Empire attracted fifth- and sixth-century raiders – the Slavs from the northwest, the Avars from the north and the Sassanid Persians from the southeast. But in 647 came a new and very different threat as Muhammed's newly converted Arab warriors advanced to the very gates of Constantinople and were only finally defeated after a four-year siege. A second invasion in 717–18 brought much of eastern Antaolia under Islamic rule for the first time.

Christianity was tolerated, but Christians endured severe civic disabilities (including paying more tax), so many chose to convert. Others adopted the iconoclastic beliefs of Islam, gouging out the faces on frescoes and mosaics or covering them with strictly geometric designs. In 866, Byzantium began to fight back under Basil I, first of the so-called Macedonian Dynasty, and during the rule of Basil II (976–1025) had recovered most of its possessions. But by that time, Islam was here to stay.

The Seljuks

In 1071 came a new threat from the Asian steppes, the Seljuk Turks who routed a Byzantine army and captured the emperor at the Battle of Manzikert, swallowing up half their empire and setting up their own empire, the Sultanate of Rum, based at Konya. This crucially took control of several key Mediterranean ports, including Alanya and Antalya, and much of the Silk Road, along which they built a series of *kervansarays* (inns), bridges and roads that offered advanced facilities to travellers who could cross their lands in safety and comfort. Their rule was in many ways a golden age, but it proved very short-lived, as the sultanate's forces were shattered by an Ilkhanid Mongol army in 1243, plunging Anatolia into turmoil.

The Crusades

Meanwhile, Byzantium was in trouble all round. Armenia, partitioned between Arabs, Seljuks and Byzantium, emerged into independence until crushed by the Mongols in 1236. In the west, the sight of Muslims controlling the Holy Land was too much for Catholics to bear. Crusader armies gathered and began docking in Byzantine ports and tramping across Byzantine lands, helping themselves to anything they wanted along the way. As Latin princes won lands that had once been Byzantine, they held onto them and set up their own kingdoms in Jerusalem, Antioch (modern Antakya) and Edessa (modern Şanlıurfa). By 1203, the Fourth Crusade, goaded by Greek-hating Venetian doge Enrico Dandolo, stopped halfway and sacked Constantinople instead of Jerusalem; the emperors fled to Nicaea and only got their city back in 1261.

Crusaders sack Constantinople

The Ottoman Empire

As the Seljuks battled the Mongols during the 1220s, a small band of warriors led by Ertuğrul Gazi and his son Osman helped them, and in return received a grant of land, the kernel of a new empire (the Ottoman) with its first capital, from 1326, in Bursa. Within a century the Aegean and Mediterranean coasts, along with the interior and Thrace,

Piri Reis

Piri Reis (full name Hadji Muhiddin Piri Ibn Hadji Mehmed; c.1465–1555) was an Ottoman admiral, explorer and cartographer – Nelson, Columbus and Ptolemy rolled into one – best known for his magnificent world maps (1513 and 1528). There is a small museum dedicated to him in his home town of Gelibolu (see page 30).

came under Ottoman rule.

In 1453, Sultan Mehmet II took Constantinople by siege, and changed its name to İstanbul. The Ottoman Empire expanded rapidly and arrived at its golden age during the lengthy reign of Süleyman the Magnificent (1520–66), who not only doubled the size of the empire, but together with his great architect, Sinan, left Turkey a legacy of many of its finest buildings, notably its distinctive mosques.

Unfortunately many of his successors were not as competent, and the arcane details of succession to the throne often entailed fratricide or incarceration of surplus princes, and winning candidates who were barely sane. Over the centuries the great empire slowly shrank and grew decadent, increasingly menaced by its praetorian guard of janissary slave-converts, recruited from Balkan Christians. Finally, in 1825, Sultan Mahmut II had this corps abolished (with 5,000 of them massacred), founded a regular army, and began other reforms. But Serbia, Greece and Egypt declared independence, the empire was only saved from Russia during the Crimean War by French and British intervention, and another 1877 war with Russia resulted in massive territorial losses.

From Yount Turks to Atatürk's Republic

From the 1860s onwards, Ottoman dissidents began pressing for a constitutional monarchy; after the 1876 constitution was suppressed by Sultan Abdülhamid II, more radical successors – the so-called Young Turks – arose. In 1908, they established a revolutionary junta but soon led the Ottoman Empire into World War as one of the Central Powers. The war proved a disaster for the Ottomans, except for the thwarted Allied invasion at Gallipoli in 1915 – the defence led by a hitherto unknown colonel, Mustafa Kemal. Defeat in 1918 was followed by the punitive Treaty of Sèvres, which detached Otttoman territory in favour of various Allies, leaving a rump Turkish state.

The treaty – and subsequent Greek landings at Smyrna (İzmir) on the Aegean coast – sparked a national resistance movement, commanded by Gallipoli hero commander Kemal and nullifying the sultan's authority. During the ensuing War of Independence, the current frontiers of modern Turkey (ignoring Kurdish and Armenian claims) were established, and all foreign armies chased out, ending with the burning of Smyrna in September 1922. The 1923 Treaty of Lausanne recognised these gains and officially exchanged 1.5 million Greek Orthodox residents in Anatolia with 400,000 Muslims in Greece.

Kemal Atatürk

Kemal became president of the new Turkish Republic, and set about transforming society by abolishing polygamy, the fez, the turban, dervish orders and other religious brotherhoods, while introducing compulsory education and suffrage for women, a uniform law code, a Latin script, the Gregorian calendar and surnames – for himself he chose Atatürk.

Recent History

Neutral in World War II, Turkey then emerged as NATO member and US client state, while developing slowly into a multi-party democracy. The military, however, has always stood by to ensure that all regimes conform to Atatürk's secularist ideals, with four coups of varying fashions between 1960 and 1997. In 1974, Turkey invaded northern Cyprus in support of the island's Muslim minority, increasing tensions with Greece (only now abated) and helping to stymie its attempts to join the EU. Another irritant for outside observers is Turkey's human-rights record, particularly in relation to journalists, religious/ethnic minorities and especially the Kurds – an ongoing Kurdish rebellion since 1984 has resulted in over 40,000 deaths on all sides.

But since the 2002 coming to power of the Islamist AK government, the country (especially its tourism sector) has been booming, the power of the army has been curtailed and necessary EU-compliant civil reforms have inched forward. Whether as a future EU member (negotiations are stalled) or a current major regional power and member of the G20, Turkey is once again a country to be reckoned with.

A face of modern Turkey

Historical Landmarks

c. 3600BC Troy founded on the north Aegean coast.

c. 1250–1210BC Troy falls to Greeks; Hittite empire collapses.

1200–800 BC Sea Peoples, Phrygians, Lydians, Greeks colonise Anatolia.

546BC Persian King Cyrus II conquers Anatolia.

334–323BC The campaigns of Alexander the Great.

4th–2nd centuries BC Era of the Hellenistic city-states.

130BC Roman province of Asia Minor created.

AD325 First ecumenical council at Nicaea codifies Christian belief.

330 Constantine inaugurates capital at Constantinople (Byzantium).

647–717 Arab invasions introduce Islam to Anatolia.

1071 Seljuk Turks rout Byzantine army at Manzikert.

1204 Latin Crusaders sack and occupy Constantinople.

1243 Seljuk empire defeated by the Ilkhanid Mongols.

1326 Ottomans take Bursa, which becomes their first capital.

1453 Ottoman Sultan Mehmet II conquers Constantinople.

1520–66 Reign of Süleyman the Magnificent.

1877–1913 Accelerated decline of the Ottoman Empire.

1908 Young Turk Revolution abolishes sultan's absolute power.

1914–18 Ottomans fight World War I as a German ally.

1919–22 Gallipoli hero Mustafa Kemal leads War of Independence.

1923 Republic of Turkey established with Kemal as president.

1924–38 Kemal, as Atatürk, imposes secularisation and modernisation.

1946 Turkey comes under American tutelage.

1950 First free elections, won by Adnan Menderes.

1960 Menderes deposed by first military coup.

1974 Turkey invades northern Cyprus.

1983 Return to civilian government under Turgut Özal.

1984 Kurdish PKK launches guerilla insurrection in southeast.

1999 Earthquake kills thousands in northwest Turkey.

2002 Islamist AK Party forms majority government.

2005 Negotiations begin on Turkey joining the EU.

2007 Second AK electoral victory despite military intimidation.

2011 Third AK victory, but insufficient majority to rewrite constitution.

WHERE TO GO

The Turkish Coast stretches all the way from Thrace and the Dardanelles to Antakya near the Syrian border. This section focuses on the areas most popular with western tourists, covering the entire Aegean, and the Mediterranean as far east as Alanya. The chapter divisions take in all the main resorts as well as excursions to ancient sites.

THE NORTH AEGEAN

Known today as the Dardanelles, but to the ancients as the Hellespont, these straits, only 1,200m (3,937ft) wide at their narrowest point, mark the division of Europe and Asia, and the Sea of Marmara (the ancient Propontus) from the Aegean. They have proved a strategic and romantic challenge to both military heroes and brave fools. Leander swam across by night to visit his lover, Hero; English poet Lord Byron swam across for fun in 1810. The Persian army, led by Xerxes, crossed the straits on a bridge of boats in 480BC in a failed bid to conquer Greece; Alexander crossed in 334BC to defeat the Persians. The north shore comprises the Gallipoli Peninsula; on the south flank stands Troy. This is truly a fitting introduction to a coast of legends.

Gallipoli (Gelibolu)

Those who are not military history buffs might shy away from visiting **Gallipoli**, but anyone who comes here will be moved by the immense tragedy and dignity of the story told throughout this beautiful and now peaceful peninsula. In late 1914 and early 1915, at the instigation of an inexperienced

Left: Poppies in Pergamon

Winston Churchill, in his first major role as First Lord of the Admiralty, the British and French made several attempts to force the Dardanelles and sail a fleet to Constantinople, but were repulsed by Ottoman mines with heavy losses. Subsequently, on 25 April 1915, the Allies made a dawn landing on the Gallipoli peninsula to overcome Ottoman land defenses. General Liman von Sanders, the German commander of the Ottoman armies, deputised local operations to a brilliant, ruthless young Turkish officer, Mustafa Kemal (later Atatürk). 'I am not ordering you to attack, I am ordering you to die,' he proclaimed to his poorly equipped troops. And they did in droves during the first days of the campaign, halting the Allied advance inland and buying time for reinforcements to arrive. Some 46,000 Allied troops and 86,000 Turkish troops were killed, and hundreds of thousands more were injured on both sides, before the Allies withdrew in de-

Turkish War Memorial at Morto Bay

feat late in 1915. Many of the Allied casualties came from the Australian and New Zealand Army Corps (ANZAC), and Anzac Day (25th April) is still commemorated locally by both countries.

There are numerous guided tours of the peninsula from Çanakkale and Eceabat, or you can explore the region on your own. Much of the scenic peninsula is now a national park, rich in plant and bird life. A good general orientation is available at the moving **Kabatepe Military Museum**, 9km northwest of Eceabat near the west coast (9am–1pm & 2–6pm; charge). Of the many well-tended cemeteries, cenotaphs and other memorial plaques that mark the former battlefields, the most famous are the **Lone Pine Cemetery**, the **Nek** and **Anzac Cove**, where Australian and New Zealand troops are buried, as well as **Çonkbayırı**, scene of the fiercest battles, Kemal's most famous exploits and both

Side by side

'There is no difference between the Johnnies and the Mehmets to us,
Where they lie side by side here in this country of ours…
You, the mothers who sent their sons from faraway countries, wipe away your tears;
Your sons are now lying in our bosom and are in peace after having lost their lives on this land
They have become our sons as well.'

Atatürk's eulogy to the fallen at Gallipoli

Anzac and Turkish memorials. The British and French landings were in the far south at Cape Helles and Morto Bay respectively; tours tend not to visit these.

Also on the peninsula, 50km (34 miles) from most of the battlefields, is the historic port town of **Gelibolu** where a Byzantine tower on the old port is home to **Piri Reis Museum**
museum (daily except Thur 8.30am–noon, 1–5pm; free) dedicated to the great Ottoman cartographer (see page 22).

Çanakkale and Turkey's Aegean islands

Ferries cross frequently between Eceabat or Kilitbahir and
Çanakkale, on the southeast shore of the Dardanelles. The
largest town in the region and a good base for exploring, it
has some reasonable hotels, a pleasant promenade with great
views across the straits and a few seafood restaurants. About
1km (½ mile) from the centre, the 15th-century Ottoman fort

Çanakkale

is closed to the public, though next door a small **Naval Museum** features a replica of the mine-layer *Nusrat* which frustrated Allied naval attempts to run the Dardanelles (Tue–Wed, Fri–Sun 9am–noon, 1.30–5pm; charge; fortress grounds daily 9am–10pm in summer; 9am–5pm in winter). The **Archaeology Museum** (1.5km/1 mile south of the centre on the Troy road; daily summer 8am–6.45pm, winter 8am–5.30pm; charge) contains many local finds, in particular two intricately carved sarcophagi.

From Çanakkale, Kabatepe dock or Geyikli İskelesi near Troy, car ferries or faster sea-buses make short trips to **Gökçeada (İmroz)** and Bozcaada (Tenedos), Turkey's two largest Aegean islands. They each have volcanic origins, excellent south-coast beaches and a historically Greek-Orthodox population, but there the resemblance ends. Gökçeada is much bigger, with more dramatic scenery and a few hundred Greeks still living in the remotest villages; their summer festival, often lacking in Greece itself, when the island diaspora returns from Greece, İstanbul or even further afield to re-occupy ancestral homes. Public transport is sparse, so it's definitely worth taking a rental car across. **Bozcaada** has an architecturally exquisite port town, a trendy İstanbul clientele which pushes prices up, and excellent wines from local vineyards. A superb castle (daily 10am–1pm & 2–6pm; charge) modified by every successive power in the Aegean guards the port. Less than twenty Greek Orthodox remain, and unlike on Gökçeada there are no priests, or religious services.

Troy

For centuries, people thought Homer's stories of the siege of **Troy** and the voyages of Odysseus to be pure myth, but while the tales of gods and monsters can perhaps be taken with a pinch of salt, *The Iliad* and *The Odyssey* have some basis in fact. According to Homer, Paris, son of King Priam of Troy, kidnapped Helen, wife of King Menelaos of Sparta, the most beautiful woman in the world, and took her as his wife. Menelaos, his brother King Agamemnon, and an army of Greeks including the great heroes Achilles, Hector and Odysseus, set sail with an armada of 1,000 ships, laying siege to Troy for many years. Eventually they came up with the idea of a wooden horse left as a gift outside the gate. The overly trusting Trojans wheeled it into the city, but that night, Greek soldiers crept from its belly and opened the gates. And so the war was won, and the phrase 'Beware of Greeks bearing gifts' born.

It was 1871 before German-American archaeologist Heinrich Schliemann discovered the site that he claimed to be Troy, 32km (20 miles) south from Çanakkale (daily 8am–7pm in summer; 8am–5pm in winter; charge). It is a complicated

Detail of the Temple of Athena, found in Troy

place to visit, with at least nine city layers spanning some 4,000 years. The map/guide on sale at the entrance, or handily posted map-placards, help make sense of the site. Schliemann's greatest find, a large horde of gold, silver and copper treasure that he attributed to King Priam, was in fact nearly 1,000 years older. It vanished from Berlin in 1945, courtesy of the Red Army, and turned up in Moscow in 1993; it's

Behramkale

now in the Pushkin Museum, the focus of a three-way legal wrangle for ownership between Germany, Turkey and Russia.

Behramkale (Assos)

Popular amongst İstanbul trendies long before Bozcaada, **Behramkale**, on the Gulf of Edremit, 70km (40 miles) south of Troy, is one of the prettiest villages on the Turkish coast. With no beach and a protected architectural environment, its touristic development has been modest, confined to a handful of small hotels, some in converted acorn warehouses, both down at the tiny port and in the upper village some 240m (785ft) up the cliff. Upper Behramkale is dominated by the acropolis of ancient **Assos** (daily 8.30am–sunset; charge) with its stupendous views across to the Greek island of Lésvos, from where colonists founded the city in the 10th century BC. From 348 to 345BC, Aristotle lived here as the guest of ruler Hermias, while St Paul passed through in about AD55. Highlight of the acropolis

is the 6th-century BC Temple of Athena, currently being restored with stone from the original quarries to replace the ill-advised concrete columns erected some decades ago. Other prominent remains include a particularly fine necropolis and about 3km (2 miles) of the old city walls, standing 14m (46ft) high in places.

Ayvalık

At the southern end of the Gulf of Edremit, 131km (81 miles) from Behramkale. **Ayvalık** (the 'place of the quince') grew up in the 18th century as a Greek Orthodox town, but was virtually abandoned after the 1923

Old Mosque near Altinova, Ayvalik

exchange of populations. Subsequently repopulated by Muslim refugees from Crete, and Lésvos island opposite, it has grown massively but the centre still has a strong Greek flavour and immense charm, its fishing harbour overlooking a bay scattered with islets. The largest is **Cunda** (also called Alibey Adasi), with another well-preserved Greek settlement known by its founders as Moskhoníssi. Several of the Greek Orthodox churches have been converted into mosques. The area's main beach resort lies several kilometres south, at Sarımsaklı, which has little charm, but does offer good sand and watersports. The area is a major producer of olive oil.

Pergamon

Head south south of Ayvalık on Route E87 for 54km (33 miles) to **Pergamon**, once the most glamorous city in Asia ◄ **8** Minor. Although originally founded in the 8th century BC, Pergamon reached its zenith during late Hellenistic and Roman times. One of Alexander the Great's successors, Lysimakhos, entrusted a great treasure to his eunuch-steward Philetaeros. After Lysimakhos was killed in battle in 281BC, Philetaeros passed these riches on to his nephew Eumenes I, founder of the Pergamene dynasty, who used the fortune to begin a complete makeover of the city. By the second century BC Pergamon (also known as Pergamum), population 150,000, controlled almost half of Asia Minor. In 133BC, King Attalos III changed world history by bequeathing his vast territories to Rome.

The city had all the usual trimmings, but also three truly outstanding features that made it famous throughout the ancient

Medicine at the Aesclepion

According to legend, Asklepios, the son of Apollo and the nymph Koronis, was taught medicine by the centaur Khiron and became the Greek god of healing, using the blood of the Gorgon to restore slain men to life. His emblem, a snake curled about a winged staff, is still the symbol of the medical profession. His temple and 'wellness' centre at Pergamon became one of the greatest therapeutic centres in the ancient world under the masterful tutelage of Galen (c.129–202 AD), considered to be the first great physician in Western history. Treatments included sleeping in the temple of Asklepios – after which the priests would interpret your dreams – colonic irrigation and walking through a tunnel while the doctor whispered a cure in your ear, but Galen was also the first to discover that arteries carried blood. His treatments were still standard practices 1,500 years later.

world. It was a notable religious centre, mixing worship of Zeus, the emperors and exotic Egyptian deities with that of the city's patron goddess, Athena, and the normal Greek pantheon; it became a place of healing *(see page 35)*; and it had a library fit to rival the Great Library at Alexandria. In fact, rivalry between the two was so intense that the Egyptians refused to let the Pergamene have papyrus, so its scribes revived the old technique of writing on treated animal skin (parchment) and binding it into codices. In its prime, the library contained some 200,000 volumes, but in 41BC Mark Anthony gave most of it to Cleopatra as a gift, perhaps to replace the thousands of scrolls that went up in flames when Julius Caesar inadvertently set fire to Alexandria in 48BC.

There are two distinct areas of ruins – the **Acropolis** (a long, steep climb from the modern town centre) and the **Asklepion**, about 8km (5 miles) apart by road; there is a taxi rank near the museum. Both sites are open daily 8.30am–5.30pm, until 6.30pm in summer (separate entrance charges).

The Asklepion visible today dates mostly from Emperor Hadrian's reign (AD117–138), with two round temples to Asklepios and his son Telesphoros, healing springs, a theatre and a library. But most of the city is on the Acropolis, 300m (1,000ft) overhead with superb 360° views. Near the highest point stand the partially restored Corinthian columns of the 2nd-century AD **Temple of Trajan and Hadrian** and its stoa, just above the scantier remains of the **Temple of Athena**. The fabulously carved Altar of Zeus, with a

Temple of Trajan and Hadrian

The Amphitheatre at Pergamon, with Bergama below

frieze depicting the battle between gods and the Titans, was mostly taken to Germany during the 1880s and is now in Berlin's Pergamon Museum, along with much of the other choice relief art from the site. The Hellenistic **theatre**, dramatically built into the hillside, could hold 10,000. It originally had a removable wooden stage to allow access to a small Temple of Dionysos, though in Roman times a stone structure was built.

Below, in the lively market town of **Bergama** with its old hill quarter, the **Kızıl Avlu** (Red Basilica; daily 8.30am–5.30pm, until 6.30pm in summer; charge) was founded in the 2nd century AD as a temple to the Egyptian gods Serapis, Harpokrates and Isis, before being converted to a Christian basilica. Its pagan days are commemorated in *Revelations 2:13*, which cites Pergamon as where 'Satan has his throne', a clear reference to the still-thriving Egyptian cult. The **Pergamon Arkeoloji Müsezi** (Archaeological Museum; İzmir Caddesi; Tue–Sun 8.30am–noon, 1–5.30pm; charge) houses those finds not taken to Berlin, as well as artefacts from the dam-threatened archaeological site of Allianoi.

Çandarlı and Foça

With limited and mediocre accommodation at Bergama, the little resort and port of **Çandarlı** some 35km (22 miles) southwest makes a good potential base with its two beaches flanking a well-restored Genoese castle. Further along the coast, the Foça Peninsula is relatively undeveloped, with long stretches of militarily-protected coastline; the few public beaches tend to have stiff entry charges.

Preparing fishing line in Foça

The town of **Eski Foça** (Old Foça), the successor of ancient Phokaea, has a wonderful setting, another renovated Genoese fortress, and a number of restored Ottoman-Greek houses. It's a popular retreat of people from Manisa and İzmir, and finding accommodation can be tricky on warm weekends.

The same cautions apply to nearby **Yeni Foça** (New Foça), with more well-restored old houses but an exposed beach. 'Phokaea' means 'seal' in ancient Greek, and a few Mediterranean monk seals still survive locally, although they are almost never seen.

THE SOUTH AEGEAN

The South Aegean is much busier with foreign visitors than the North Aegean, with a longer season, warmer sea and an embarrassment of archaeological riches. There is also more choice in shops, restaurants and hotels.

İzmir's seafront clock tower

İzmir

The third largest city in Turkey with a population of nearly 4 million, **İzmir**, formerly Smyrna, claims to be the birthplace of Homer (8th century BC), and there has been habitation here for over 5,000 years. But the city's confirmed history starts in the 4th century BC when Hellenistic generals Lysimakhos and Antigonos built a fortified settlement. Set on a huge horseshoe bay, its superb harbour, a key outlet to the Mediterranean at the end of the Silk Road, ensured that İzmir prospered. Until World War I, it was a glamorous, cosmopolitan city, where Greeks and Latins far outnumbered Muslims, but that changed during the last days of the bitter War of Independence. As the Greek army retreated in disorder and thousands of refugees converged on the docks hoping for a ship out, Smyrna fell on 9 September 1922 to Atatürk's forces, who engaged in the traditional three days of plunder and murder before setting 70 percent of the city on fire.

İzmir eventually recovered, and the seafront promenade is lined with a combination of palms, cafés and a few opulent mansions in Pounda district that survived the blaze. The pivotal **Konak Meydanı** sports a pretty little mosque, the **Konak**

Kemeraltı Bazaar

Camii (1748), the **Saat Kulesi**, a decorative clock tower built in 1901 donated by Sultan Abdül Hamit, and a monument dedicated to the first Turkish soldier to lose his life during the Greek invasion of 1919. To the south, in Turgutreis Parkı, are the city's Archaeological and Ethnographic Museums (both Tue–Sun 8.30am–5.30pm; charge). The **Arkeoloji Müzezi** has an impressive collection of finds from nearby sites, including some fine Classical statuary, while the **Etnografya Müzesi**, housed in a restored late-Ottoman hospital, has interesting photos and reconstructed buildings showing what the city was like pre-1922. Walk through the back streets from here and you find yourself in the **Kemeraltı bazaar**, a gloriously eclectic mix of everything from leather jackets to live chickens. Behind this, at the foot of the castle, lies the Roman **Agora** (daily 8.30am–noon, 1–5pm; charge), rebuilt by Marcus Aurelius after an earthquake in AD178.

The best views of the city are from above. Climb (or take a taxi) up to **Kadifekale** (Velvet Fortress), first built by Alexander's successors but rebuilt and used by everyone since; its final ruined incarnation is a 500-year-old Ottoman fortress. To the north, you will notice the **Kültür Parkı**, the city's main open space but also home to tea gardens and the

G ► **İzmir Tarih ve Sanat Müzesi** (History and Art Museum; Tue–Sun 8.30am–noon & 1–5.30pm; charge), a fascinating museum that includes a sumptuous collection of Hellenistic, Roman and Byzantine jewellery, along with statuary and ceramics from the 6th century BC to the Ottoman period. Just to the south of the park, the **Ahmet Piriştina Museum of** ◄ **H** **Metropolitan History and Archive** (Mon–Sat 8.30am–5.30pm; free) is a converted fire station, charting the city's history, with special reference to its fires.

To round off the day, take the brick **Asansör** (Elevator; ◄ **I** 7am–late; free), built in 1907 by a wealthy Jewish businessman, up to the old Karataş district, historically the Jewish quarter, where you can have a drink, a meal *(see page 109)* and watch the sun set over the bay.

Blue Cruising

There can be few things more perfect than drifting gently along one of the world's most beautiful coasts in a traditional wooden *gulet*, stopping to swim or dive off where you choose, sunbathe in deserted coves, or snorkel above ancient ruins toppled by an earthquake into the sea. And all this can be yours on one of Turkey's famous blue cruises. Whether you choose to go for a day or several, join a tour or hire a whole boat for your own party – the options are limitless and the prices (in spring or autumn) very affordable. Do your homework. A *gulet* traditionally sleeps between 8 and 14 people although they can be larger; is propelled largely by motor (sails are usually decorative); and comes with both sail and motor; and comes fully equipped and staffed. If you have your own boat, you can set your own itinerary, eat on board, have barbecues on the beach or berth in town for a night on the tiles, as you prefer. Many tour operators offer this as an option *(see pages 90–1)* or you can wander along any harbour and see if you can do a deal locally, although this is obviously more fraught with difficulties.

Çeşme Peninsula

Çeşme Peninsula

Pushing west into the Aegean from İzmir, the **Çeşme Peninsula** is a holiday playground for wealthy city-dwellers and savvy foreigners, with a perfect blend of great beaches, equable summer weather and natural hot springs that have spawned some ravishingly good spas.

Located some 75km (47 miles) west of İzmir on the O-30 motorway, **Çeşme** (whose name means 'wall fountain') is a pretty town with a 14th-century Genoese **Castle of St Peter** (daily 8.30am–7pm, until 5pm winter; charge) with displays of sculpture, coins and artefacts from nearby Ildırı (Erythrai) and a 16th-century *kervansaray*, built during Süleyman the Magnificent's reign and now once again a hotel. A recently opened marina is bidding to catapult Çeşme into the big leagues from its rather sleepy past.

Popular resorts on the surrounding peninsula include **Dalyan** (5km/3 miles north of Çeşme), with more yacht anchorage and famous fish restaurants; **Ilıca** (5km/3 miles east of Çeşme), which has hot springs offering therapeutic treatments as well as several excellent spa hotels; and **Alaçatı** (9km/5 miles away), a lovingly preserved former Greek village noted for its great wind- and kite-surfing, trendy nightlife and boutique hotels. The best beaches are to be found at **Altınkum**, 9km (6 miles) southwest of town, a series of sandy coves protected from over-development by the forest service.

Sardis (Sart)

Detour inland for 100km (60 miles) on route E96 from İzmir to visit **Sardis** (daily 8am–7pm, closes 5pm winter; charge),  once the richest city in Asia Minor. The capital of ancient Lydia, it lay at the junction of the roads between Ephesus, Pergamon and the east, and the Lydians profited from every passing traveller. Not only that – the mountain overhead was rich in gold. In the 6th century BC, the last of the Lydian kings, Kroisos (Croesus), invented coins and dice but his conspicuous wealth attracted unwanted attention from the Persians. Kroisos consulted the Delphic Oracle which replied that if he attacked the Persian king, Cyrus the Great, a great empire would fall. Kroisos went ahead, but unfortunately the kingdom destroyed was his own. Amongst the many ruins, highlights include the vast **Temple of Artemis**, begun in the 4th century BC but tumbled by an earthquake in AD17 before it was completed; the

Sardis gymnasium

beautifully restored **Marble Court** of the 3rd-century AD gymnasium; and the impressive, reconstructed **synagogue**, the largest ancient synagogue outside of Palestine, evidence of the sizeable, prosperous Jewish community in Roman Sardis.

Selçuk

14 ▶ Although first settled almost 4,000 years ago, **Selçuk** only really began to grow after the harbour of nearby Ephesus finally silted up in the 5th century AD. These days it is a small provincial town with a few interesting sites. The **Selçuk Museum** (main through road; daily 8.30am–5pm, until 6.30pm in summer; charge) is home to many of the finds from Ephesus and other nearby sites, including sumptuous statues of the 'many-breasted' Artemis and a playful bronze statuette of Eros riding a dolphin.

On **Ayasoluk Hill**, above the town, is an ancient citadel. It was here, in about AD 100, that St John the Evangelist, one of Christ's twelve apostles, supposedly died and was buried. In the 6th century AD, Emperor Justinian built a magnificent **basilica** around his tomb (daily 8am–5pm, until 6.30pm summer; charge). This was destroyed by the Mongols in 1402, but the place is still an important Christian pilgrimage site. At the foot of the hill is the ornate, late 14th-century **İsa Bey Mosque** (daily 9am–6pm).

On the way out of town, heading towards Ephesus, pause briefly next to a few bits of fallen marble and one column, all that remain of the once-glorious **Temple of Artemis** (daily 8.30am–

> ### Deliverance
>
> During persecutions under Roman Emperor Decius (r. 249–51 AD), seven Christians took refuge in a cave a few hundred metres east of Ephesus and fell asleep. When they woke up and returned to town, they found that 200 years had passed, Christianity had become the state religion and they were safe.

5.30pm; free), once considered among the Seven Wonders of the ancient world. First built in the 7th century BC to honour Cybele, burnt in 356 BC by a lunatic, rebuilt by Alexander's successors and sacked by the Goths in AD263, its masonry was eventually plundered by Justinian for recycling in İstanbul's Aya Sofya and Selçuk's St John's Basilica.

Ephesus theatre, at the end of the Arcadian Way

Ephesus

In Roman times, **Ephesus** (3km/2 miles west of Selçuk; daily 8am–6.30pm, closes 5.30pm in winter; charge) was the jewel of the Aegean coast. A dazzling city founded by Athenian settlers in about 1000BC, it thrived on the profits from its harbour, only eventually withering when its harbour silted up in the 5th century AD; it now lies several kilometres inland. St Paul lived and preached here in AD52, and later wrote one of his New Testament epistles to the Ephesians.

The site is extensive, extraordinarily well preserved and well restored. To do things the easy way, take a taxi from the main car park at the bottom to the Magnesian Gate and East Gymnasium at the top of the site and walk downhill along the Street of Curetes past the Upper Agora, Trajan's Fountain and the Odeon, a 'studio' theatre for concerts and poetry. The small 2nd-century AD **Temple of Hadrian** with an ornate façade is further down on the right, with the **Baths of Scholastica** behind it – look out for the communal toilets and beautifully draped, headless statue of the bath's benefactor. Opposite are a large mosaic and steps leading up to the late Roman and early Byzantine **terrace houses** (daily 8am–6pm, closes 5pm winter; separate charge) decorated with frescoes and mosaics.

On the corner with Marble Avenue, the city's **brothel** is signed by a footprint in the stone. Inside, rooms surrounding the central atrium have decoration that suit the purpose while in the main reception area is a mosaic of the Four Seasons. Just off Marble Avenue, on the left, the superbly restored **Library of Celsus** was built early in the 2nd century AD by the Roman Consul Gaius Julius Aquila and destroyed by Goths in AD 262. Between times, it housed some 12,000 scrolls.

Library of Celsus detail

Further on, the 24,000-seat **theatre** stands at one end of the **Arcadian Way**, the colonnaded main street down to the harbour. It was so sophisticated that by the 5th century AD, its covered walkways had street lamps at night (along with only Rome and Antioch). Just north of the Arcadian Way stand the huge 2nd-century AD Harbour Baths and Gymnasium and the Church of the Virgin Mary, the first ever dedicated to the Virgin, converted from a Roman warehouse. On the far side of Marble Avenue are sparse remains of the **stadium** and the Vedius Gymnasium.

An old legend claimed that the Virgin Mary came to Ephesus with St John and lived her last days here. In the early 19th century, a German nun, Catherine Emmerich, had a vision of her house and in 1891, some Lazarist monks found a house that matched. In 1967, Pope Paul VI arrived

Camel wrestling

One of the hottest spectator sports in the southern Aegean is camel-wrestling, with a circuit of about 30 festivals, and some 100 camels competing at any given time. Based on the mating-season rituals of wild camels, individual matches last 10 minutes, with a huge amount of surrounding razzmatazz. The season lasts from December to February.

and declared it authentic. Today, the **Meryemana** (Virgin Mary's House; 5km (3 miles) south of Ephesus; 7.30am–sunset; charge) is a major pilgrimage site, with religious services on 15 August and the first Sunday of October.

Kuşadası

About 20km (12 miles) southwest of Selçuk, **Kuşadası** is the most popular resort in the South Aegean, with a crowded marina as well as a busy cruise terminal, plus plenty of shops, restaurants and bars. The only sights are the 14th-century Genoese castle on **Güvercin Adası** (Pigeon Island), with snack-bars and tea gardens inside, and the 16th-century **Kervansaray** by the harbour, now back in service as a hotel. There are no beaches in town, but there are several nearby: the best are Tusan and Pamucak, a few kilometres north.

Just 33km (20 miles) to the south, the **Dilek Yarımadası Milli Parkı** (daily summer 8am–6.30pm, must exit 7pm; charge) is a stunningly beautiful 27,000-ha (66,700-acre) national park encompassing Samsun Daği (the ancient Mt Mykale), with fine

Shopping in Kuşadası

beaches, woodlands, and wildlife including jackals, boar and badgers.

Steam buffs may want to take a detour a short distance inland to the **Çamlık Buharlı Lokomotif Müzesi** (Steam Locomotive Museum; daily 8.30am–5.30pm; charge), home to some 25 pre-World War II trains from all over Europe.

Priene, Miletus and Didyma

On the south flanks of Samsun Dağı, 37km (23 miles) from Kuşadası, **Priene** (daily 8.30am–6.30pm, closes 5.30pm winter; charge) has one of the finest settings of any ancient city in Anatolia, on a series of pine-clad terraces backed by huge cliffs with views across the flood-plain of the Menderes River. Moved here from elsewhere in the region during the 5th century BC, Priene was still one of the first local cities to have its port silt up, before the Romans arrived, so the architecture and layout retains its Ionian/Hellenistic purity. There is a marked route through the grid of streets, past houses and shops, council buildings, the agora, Temple of Zeus and Temple of Athena (designed by Pytheos, architect of Bodrum's Mausoleum, *see page 53*), the theatre and the Sanctuary of Demeter.

Carry on south for another 22km (14 miles) and you reach the next of the great city-states that once traded along this coast, **Miletus** (Milet; Tue–Sun 8.30am–5.30pm, until 7pm in summer; charge). Settled by a mythical son of King Kodros in the 10th century BC, it became hugely rich, with colonies in Egypt and the south of France, and was the birthplace of Thales, considered to be the first of the great Greek philosophers and astronomer-mathematicians in the 6th century BC, noted for his advocacy of scientific rather than mythological explanations of natural phenomena. Relatively little of the city remains, but the huge theatre, with seating for 25,000, is in astonishing condition.

Nearby **Didyma** (Didim; 15km/9 miles further along the same road; daily summer 9am–7.30pm, winter 8am–5.30; charge) is best visited towards sunset when the light glows through the columns of its superb **Temple of Apollo**, home to one of the great oracles of the ancient world, second in importance only to Delphi. Work on this vast marble temple went on for a full 800 years after Alexander the Great sponsored its reconstruction (it had been destroyed by the Persians), but it was never completed. Now the whole of the surrounding area, especially the beach town of **Altınkum**  20

Miletus' amphitheatre

5km (3 miles) south, has been overwhelmed by building work as developers cash in on the desire of northern Europeans to own a little piece of sunshine.

Excursions to Aphrodisias and Pamukkale

Priene and Miletus originally stood well to seaward of the advancing delta of the Menderes River, known in Classical times as the Maeander (giving us the verb we still use today). Follow it inland along Route E87 to **Aphrodisias** (80km/50 miles from the coast; daily summer 8am–6.30pm, closes 5.30pm winter; charge), a vast city devoted in antiquity to marble sculpture and the love goddess. Most of the ruins date from the 1st and 2nd centuries AD and include a magnificent theatre, 30,000-seat stadium – one of the best preserved in Anatolia – the Tetrapylon (quadruple gateway) and colonnades of the Temple of Aphrodite, later converted into a

A frieze block in Aphrodisias

Christian basilica. The site museum (may close Mon) features abundant local sculpture.

A further 90km (56 miles) northeast by roundabout roads lies one of the world's most stunning geological formations, the so-called 'Cotton Castle' at **Pamukkale** (24hr; charge during daylight hours), an extraordinary solidified cascade of travertine formed by mineral-rich hot springs, its chalk-white basins and pool water glimmering and changing with the light. There is a village, Pamukkale Köyü, at the base of the travertines, but atop the plateau you will also find the huge ruined city of **Hierapolis**, founded by Eumenes II of Pergamon, which grew rich from the wool trade and as a spa. It had a large large Jewish and later Christian community but was virtually destroyed during the Arab invasions of the 7th century. Prominently on view are a fine Roman theatre, still used for performances, and a huge necropolis, where the most sumptuous tomb belonged to one Flavius Zeuxis.

Pammukkale

Only one of several paths can be used at any given time to traverse the deilciate travertine terraces, to protect them from erosion, but take your swimming costume along so you can have a dip in the Antique Pool (daily 8am–7pm; charge), the once-sacred bathing area of the spa (said to be good for arthritic complaints). Most of the larger tourist hotels and many other spas are a few kilometres away in the village of Karakhayıt.

THE TURQUOISE COAST

Bodrum

A playground for Turks and foreigners alike, this southwestern corner of Anatolia, where the Aegean and the Mediterranean meet, has relatively little in the way of high culture and ancient artefacts but compensates with stunning scenery, fabulous beaches, sybaritic resorts and clear blue waters that delight yachties, divers and windsurfers.

23 Party central is **Bodrum**, 125km (78 miles) southeast of Didyma. Bodrum's name means 'cellar' or 'dungeon' and it was used as a place of exile by both the Ottomans and republican Turkey; these days, it one of the most liberal and gay-friendly towns in Turkey, sophisticated and worldy enough to seem a transplanted piece of the French Riviera. Architectural rules have kept the town fairly small and low-slung, its houses piled around its two bays like sugar cubes. If you book a hotel here, you may well be staying in one of a dozen resort villages that encircle the indented Bodrum pensinsula, 40 minutes' drive distant, as there are relatively few big hotels in Bodrum proper.

Founded in the 12th century BC as Halikarnassos, in the 4th century BC it was ruled by King Mausolus of the Carians, whose sister/wife, Artemesia II, built him a tomb so grand that

Herodotus

Named the 'Father of History' by Cicero and, less flatteringly, the 'Father of Lies' by his detractors, Herodotus lived in Halikarnassos (modern Bodrum) from c.484–425BC. He was the first person known to collect, collate and publish his material systematically and objectively, publishing *The Histories* in nine volumes: a chronicle of the 5th-century Persian Wars, along with a wealth of strange travellers' tales reported by returning sailors.

the **Mausoleum** (Tue–Sun 9am–5pm; charge) became one of the Seven Wonders of the ancient world and the prototype for all other mauseolea. It stood nearly 50m (160ft) high, with 250,000 stones and surrounded by grand friezes, but only fragments of it now remain, and most of the best reliefs are in the British Museum. Just to the north is the ancient **theatre** (Tue–Sun 8.30am–5.30pm; charge), recently restored and back in use for the September festival. Once seating more than 13,000, most of it was destroyed by an earthquake, with the masonry (like that of the Mausoleum) re-used to build the castle, and the new version has a cosier capacity of 1,000.

The **Castle of St Peter** (Tue–Sun 8.30am–5.30pm, summer until 6.30pm, but different opening times for the separate exhibits inside; charges), built in the 15th century by the Knights of St John, is a magnificent fortress that was for 70 years until 1522 a lone, heavily fortified outpost of militant Christianity in Anatolia. It is now home to a world-class Museum of Underwater Archaeology, whose treasures include a 14th-century BC shipwreck in the Uluburun Wreck Hall, an 11th-century AD Byzantine ship and its cargo in the Glass Wreck Hall, and the richly endowed

Bodrum's castle casting reflections

Looking towards Myndus from Gumuşluk

tomb of a Carian princess, whom some say might have been the last Carian queen Ada, dating to about 330 BC.

Bodrum Peninsula Resorts

An ever-expanding ribbon of hotels, apartments and villas envelop the peninsula that stretches out southwest and north-west of Bodrum, but the different resorts do have distinct identities. **Gümbet** is popular with party-loving youngsters from the UK, while **Bitez** next along attracts an older crowd and watersports enthusiasts. **Karaincir** further west has one of the best beaches, while neighbouring **Akyarlar** is famous for its fish tavernas. **Gumuşluk**, atop ancient Myndos, combines posh with Turkish-bohemian and a decent beach, while **Yalıkavak** is more middle of the road. **Türkbükü** is very trendy, very expensive and mostly Turk-patronised, **Gölköy** is slightly 'alternative', while **Turgutreis** is by contrast the busiest, most mass-market centre.

The Road to Marmaris

As the fish swims, Marmaris isn't that far, but by land it takes a few hours to twist around the eminently scenic, statutorily protected Gulf of Gökova, with the highway passing small roadside stalls selling forest honey and olive oil.

Stop for a look at **Milas**, beyond Bodrum's airport, home to a distinctive style of carpet, some fine old Ottoman architecture and an excellent Tuesday market; and **Muğla**, the local provincial capital, its back streets filled with centuries-old Ottoman houses, the narrow lanes of its bazaar still divided by trade.

Marmaris and Around

In 1522, Süleyman the Magnificent anchored the entire Turkish fleet in **Marmaris** harbour prior to besieging Rhodes, and in 1798 Lord Nelson rested the whole British fleet here en route to Egypt to defeat Napoleon's armada at the Battle of the Nile. The deep inlet still offers some of the best anchorage on the coast, and is home to Turkey's largest marina. Marmaris has a small **castle** near the bazaar (ideal for souvenir shopping), built originally by the Knights of St John, taken over by the Ottomans and now housing a small museum (Tue–Sun 8.30am–noon, 1–5.30pm; charge). On the main road 9km (6 miles) before Marmaris is a superior, private archaeology and ethnography museum, the **Halıcı Ahmet Urkay Müzesi** (daily 9am–6pm; charge), complete with carpet and craft shops.

But most people come to Marmaris for the sun, sea,

Marmaris

watersports and nightlife, the latter found in the town centre 'Bar Street', or in the resort hotels and clubs that stretch out along the beaches of **Içmeler** and **Turunç** around the bay. Those looking for more peace and quiet head further south-west onto the remote **Bozburun Peninsula** where wonderful little boutique hotels and small villages are relatively undiscovered amidst wild mountains and increasingly narrow (though mostly paved) roads.

Out on its own peninsula, 70km (43 miles) from Marmaris, **Datça**, once just a market town and local port, has become a minor resort and real-estate centre. To the west – reachable by excursion boat from Datça as well as by land – lie the region's most idyllic beaches, at Hayit Bükü, Ova Bükü and Palamut Bükü. Beyond the latter awaits the area's only major archaeological site, partly excavated ancient

Sea Turtles

Loggerhead turtles (*Caretta caretta*) mate in the open sea during the spring migration. The huge females, who can weigh up to 180kg (400lb) and measure up to 1m (3ft) long, haul themselves ashore at one of the 17 Turkish where they themselves were born, between May and September, to lay clutches of up to 100 leathery ping-pong ball-sized eggs in the hot sand. These take seven weeks to hatch – assuming foxes do not dig them up – with the hatchlings cued to head for the water by moon- or star-light glinting on the waves. Thus, hotel and bar lights, or even torches, can disorientate them and lure them inland to die. These days, most turtle beaches are off-limits at night during breeding season, and you may see markers guarding the nests to stop you spearing them with beach umbrellas.

If they make it to adulthood (unlikely, as threats abound by sea as well) a loggerhead will usually live well past 50 years and can reach 70 years of age. They are mainly carnivorous, living on small fish, jellyfish and other marine invertebrates.

Knidos

Knidos, formerly home to a famous Aphrodite shrine. Of  this little remains; content yourself instead with a fine theatre and two Byzantine basilicas, one preserving mosaics.

Dalyan

From Marmaris, Highway 400 leads north, then east most of the 88km (54 miles) to **Dalyan**, the next resort of note. This quiet little town lies on a reed-lined river, the Dalyan Cayı, partway between Lake Köyceğiz and the sea. There are no sites within the town itself, although there are fine views of some 4th-century BC Lycian-style rock tombs in the cliff opposite. Most activities involve long, leisurely trips on the river in one of the many boats that vie for your custom along the central quays.

Upstream **Lake Köyceğiz** is open brackish water fringed in parts by reed beds where storks and herons fish. Up to 180 species of birds can be seen here seasonally when migrants stop to join the local residents, and there are plenty of butterflies, dragonflies and other wildlife including fish (*dalyan* means fishing weir), including excellent gilthead bream and sea bass which end up on restaurant plates. On the lake's south shore, are mineral-rich **thermal springs** at Sultaniye and **mud baths** at Ilıca closer to Dalyan, claimed therapeutic for a raft of nervous, digestive, dermatological and sexual disorders. After coating yourself in mud or wallowing in a 40°C domed pool, you are more than ready for the next part of the day.

Downstream, the river twists its way towards the sea, past the ruins of ancient **Kaunos** (daily dawn to dusk; charge), first settled by the Carians of Halikarnassos in the 9th century BC. Various cultures controlled it over the centuries, leaving their monumental mark, from imposing Lycian-style rock tombs, to Hellenistic walls and a theatre, Roman baths and a Byzantine basilica. Signposting and weeding have improved greatly in recent years, making the site increasingly rewarding.

River-boat trips (and a more roundabout road for drivers) both end at **İstuzu Beach** (charge for all arrivals), a superb 3.5km (2.5-mile) long sandbar that fringes the vast wetlands behind, shared by happy sunbathers during the day and loggerhead turtles *(see page 56)* who heave themselves ashore by night to lay their eggs. There are strict laws protecting the nests and the beach is closed at night during nesting season.

THE LYCIAN COAST

From Dalyan, the main highway runs southeast to Fethiye for nearly 70km (43 miles) with relatively little to excite the visitor other than the turnings for **Sarıgerme** beach and yachting-friendly, largely beach-free resort of **Göcek**. This all changes as you enter ancient Lycia (*Likya* in Turkish), with its rugged mountain soaring to over 3000m (9750 ft) elevation at two points, with only one major river valley to interrupt their climb from the sea. Until the late 1970s there was no continuous paved road through here, and most coastal settlements were easiest reached by sea. Such logistics are now history but this is still probably the most spectacularly beautiful area of the Turkish coast as well as one of the richest in history.

Fethiye

Lycia's main market and real-estate town, **Fethiye** expands  continually northeast along the coastal plain. The town, previously called Meğri or Makri, was renamed Fethiye during the 1930s, in honour of a World War I Ottoman pilot, Fethi Bey, who crashed in the Syrian desert. It was devasted by an earthquake in 1857, and after another earthquake in 1957 much of it had to be rebuilt. However, there are some fine **Lycian rock tombs** in the cliff above town, in particular the 4th-century BC Tomb of Amyntas (take the steps from Kaya Caddesi, behind the bus station; daily 8.30am– sunset; charge) and several freestanding tombs scattered round the town – most of what remains of ancient Telmessos. It also has a partly excavated Hellenistic theatre and a newly revamped **museum** (off Atatürk Caddesi; Tue–Sun 8.30am–noon & 1–5pm; charge) filled with finds from the nearby sites. A ruined **castle** with contribu-

The Lycian coast

Beach clubs

There are relatively few big beaches along this stretch of coast and many of the small inlets and coves are hard to get to. If you are not staying at a resort hotel with bathing platforms you may like to check out one of the beach clubs – a place to swim and sunbathe by day, with swimming platforms, pools, sunbeds, drinks and snacks, transforming into restaurants and dance clubs by night.

tions from many eras looms overhead, and there is an Ottoman **hamam** (Turkish bath) in the bazaar district, a perfect place to clean off the dust of the day *(see page 95)*. There are plenty of boat trips available from the bustling harbour front; there is also a great market on Tuesday. The nearest (gravelly) beaches are in Çalış, which also has a waterpark, Sultan's Aquacity (www.sultansaquacity.com).

The closest Lycian site to Fethiye is **Kadyanda** (24hr; 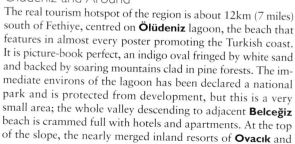 charge if warden present), 20km (12 miles) northwest on a gorgeous forested mountaintop above Üzümlü village. A loop path with signage provides a 45-minute, self-guided tour around the partly excavated city; it passes substantial chunks of city wall, a stadium with seven rows of seats, a Roman-era baths, and the theatre.

Ölüdeniz and Around

The real tourism hotspot of the region is about 12km (7 miles) south of Fethiye, centred on **Ölüdeniz** lagoon, the beach that features in almost every poster promoting the Turkish coast. It is picture-book perfect, an indigo oval fringed by white sand and backed by soaring mountains clad in pine forests. The immediate environs of the lagoon has been declared a national park and is protected from development, but this is a very small area; the whole valley descending to adjacent **Belceğiz** beach is crammed full of hotels and apartments. At the top of the slope, the nearly merged inland resorts of **Ovacık** and

Hisarönu has grown up to service a decidedly mass market and predominantly British tourist trade.

There is a wide range of watersports available off Belceğiz beach, and Baba Dağı looming overhead is Turkey's best venue for paragliding *(see page 92)*. The most popular sedate excursion is the short boat trip across to **Kelebek Vadisi** (Butterfly Valley), a steep-sided flat-bottomed valley with a waterfall inland. Some 30 species of butterfly and 40 species of moth find their way here in season (June–Sept). The properly shod and non-acrophobic can hike up and out of the valley to Faralya village up on a palisade, effectively the start of the five-week-long **Lycian Way** long-distance trail to Antalya *(see page 92)*.

Another local attraction is the enormous ghost town of **Kaya Köyü**, the largest in Asia Minor, about 5km (3 miles) northwest of Ölüdeniz. Originally Karmylassos in antiquity, this was the 3000-strong Greek village of Levissi, with three

The Lycian rock tombs

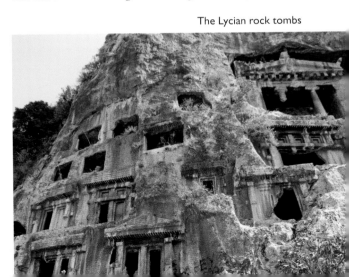

large churches, until the 1923 exchange of populations. The incoming Macedonian Muslims mostly declined to stay, considering the land on the adjoining plateau poor in comparison to what they had left. So the 600 hillside houses were mostly never re-occupied; a preservation order has been applied to the entire area, and Greek-Turkish reconciliation events have taken place here frequently.

Eşen Valley

East of Fethiye, the coast protrudes south in a fat mountainous bulge. The faster Highway 350 east cuts inland to Antalya, while the far more scenic coastal road turns south at Kemer to follow the Eşen Çayı. Sites of interest line both sides of the river valley and you need two days to visit them all. Tlos, Saklıkent and Xanthos lie on the east bank; Pinara and Letoön are to the west. The new main coastal road is busy, but the old parallel roads are ideal for cyclists in spring or autumn.

31 ➤ **Tlos** (36km/22 miles east of Fethiye; 24hr; charge when warden present) was mentioned by the Hittites in the 14th century BC, and its citadel was still inhabited by a notorious brigand,

The Goddess of Lycia

In legend, Leto was a nymph who, like so many before her, caught the eye of Zeus, ended up pregnant and fled from the wrath of his jealous wife, Hera. Arriving near the ancient Xanthos River, she was befriended by wolves (*lykoi* in Greek, conveniently, though Lycia is probably a corruption of the Hittite Lukka) who led her to the river to drink, before giving birth. Leto and her children became the presiding deities of Lycian culture, but not before the goddess had her revenge on two spiteful shepherds who had driven her away from a spring, by turning them into frogs – the ancestors perhaps of the large number of amphibians who inhabit the submerged nymphaeion today.

Saklıkent Gorge

Kanlı Ali (Bloody Ali) during the 19th century. The Roman-Byzantine city spreads below, its highlights including the apsidal hall of the Yedi Kapı baths overlooking the valley, and the imposing theatre with the Akdağ range as a backdrop.

Follow the secondary road from here through to **Saklıkent** **Gorge** (daily dawn to dusk; charge; parking charge). Some 300m (1,000ft) high and 18km (12 miles) long, this narrow canyon in the Akdağ mountains is the longest gorge in Turkey. As you approach, the road is lined with platform-restaurants overhanging the river rushing from the gorge; that is the main reason people come here – to escape the heat of the coast, have a paddle or a swim in the cold mountain water and eat trout. A prepared catwalk, and then a rocky trail (often under water) permit visitors to safely explore the lower 2km of the canyon.

The back road carries on through to **Xanthos** (1km/ ½ mile from Kınık town; daily 8am–7.30pm in summer, closes 5pm in winter; charge). This was the notional capital of the Lycian

Federation, famed for its fierce pride and independence. Twice, in 540BC when besieged by the Persian general Harpagos, and again in 42BC, when attacked by Roman legions led by Brutus, the Xanthians chose to commit mass suicide rather than surrender, the warriors making a funeral pyre for the families before heading out for a final hopeless battle. Each time, sufficient numbers appear to have survived for it to have been rebuilt, as it has a large number and variety of ruins, from a Roman theatre and mosaic-decorated Byzantine basilica to numerous fine tombs. In 1842, British archaeological scavenger Sir Charles Fellows loaded many of the finest friezes, including the originals from the 5th-century BC Harpy Tomb and the Ionic temple known as the Nereid Monument, onto the HMS *Beacon* (with the Sultan's permission) for shipment to the British Museum.

34 Across the valley from Xanthos, the **Letoön** (daily 8am–7.30pm in summer, 8.30am–5pm in winter; charge), founded in the 7th century BC, was never a city but a religious sanctuary dedicated to the goddess Leto and her twin children, Artemis and Apollo. There are three temples on the site spanning several centuries, one, dedicated to Leto, one to Apollo and one to Artemis; a French archaeological team has partially re-erected the Leto temple. The northeast entrance of the Hellenistic theatre has 16 relief masks, and a tomb with a carving of the toga-clad deceased.

Letoön

Some 21km (13 miles) north, **Pınara** (24 hr; charge when warden present) is the least visited but among the most beautifully set of the

Horse-riding on Patara's sand dunes

valley sites. Most of the city is an unexcavated jumble under pines, except for the remote theatre and a fine tomb by the seasonal stream, with a carved skyline of a town and above this a relief carving of people and animals in procession.

Patara

The oracle of Apollo once worked at **Patara** (12km/8 miles south of Xanthos; daily dawn–dusk; charge) although his temple has not yet been found amidst the dense vegetation and sand dunes here. Sun worship of a different sort is the main activity these days – Patara has one of Turkey's finest beaches, a blindingly white 15km (10-mile) long stretch of sand that has been saved from development by the presence of two ancient sites (the other being Pydnae, the port of Xanthos and the Letoön, at the far end) and turtle-nesting grounds, forcing the hotels inland to **Gelemiş** village. There are municipally run sunbeds and a reasonable snack bar

35

only at the Gelemiş end. In the village, horse-riding and canoeing on the Eşen Çayı can be arranged.

Patara was the key port of the Lycian Federation, and attracted many visitors over the years, from Alexander to Brutus, while St Nicholas was born here *(see below)*. The site, where proper excavations have only resumed since the millennium, is slowly revealing its charms: a partly submerged agora with colonnades, a bath similar to that at Tlos, a largely intact theatre cleared of drifting sand, and a fine *bouleuterion* (council house) where Lycian Federation representatives deliberated.

Kalkan

Thirteen kilometres (8 miles) east of Patara, an improved road glides down to **Kalkan**. Formerly Greek-Orthodox-in-

Baba Noël (Father Christmas)

Born in Patara in about AD270, Nicholas became Bishop of Myra, and was persecuted by Diocletian before attending Constantine's first ecumenical council at Nicaea in AD325. He is said to have saved the three daughters of a poor merchant from prostitution by anonymously tossing purses of gold coins through their window to serve as dowry. By his death in 343, his deeds ensured him a place as one of the busiest of saints, as patron saint of prisoners, sailors, travellers, unmarried girls, pawnbrokers, merchants, children, bankers, scholars, orphans, labourers, travellers, judges, paupers, victims of judicial mistakes, captives, perfumers, thieves and murderers along with many countries and cities, chief amongst them Russia and Greece. But his biggest role was yet to come, in the transformation of the 4th-century St Nicholas to Santa Claus or Father Christmas (his jolly red uniform and long white beard added by the Coca-Cola company in the 1930s to match their logo). His feast day is 6 December, when special services are held at Demre (see *page 68*).

habited Kalamaki, the post-1923 village survived from fishing, charcoal-burning and olives until the late 1970s. After a period as a bohemian retreat, Kalkan has gone decidedly upmarket, and middle-aged ex-pat, with second homes now greatly outnumbering casual accommodation. Its old centre is still attractive, with pastel-shaded old buildings climbing the slope from the yacht harbour and small pebble beach. The sea is kept

Old house in Kalkan

clean and bracing by numerous fresh-water seeps; many visitors swim from lidos flanking the sides of the bay. The nearest sandy beach is 6km (4 miles) east at **Kaputaş**, a tiny cove at the mouth of a deep gorge, reached by a long flight of steep steps off the main road. Escape the local summer heat here with a trip 8km (5 miles) inland and uphill to **İslamlar** (**Bodamya**) with its greenery and trout restaurants.

Kaş

Kaputaş is en route to **Kaş**, 30km (18 miles) east of Kalkan, **37** the main town on the south Lycian coast. This began life as the Hellenistic port of Antiphellos, exporting timber and sponges, morphing eventually into the Greek Orthodox settlement of Andifli. Unlike Kalkan it attracts a broader spectrum of both Turkish and foreign holiday-makers, with good shops along its Uzun Çarşı, good restaurants and a lively bar scene in season. The setting is stunning, the curved bay and whitewashed houses standing out in stark contrast to the orange-stained cliffs

Kaş harbour

above, while the claw-like Çukurbağ peninsula juts out west, hosting more hotels, villas and apartments. From Antiphellos remain a small Hellenistic theatre and a tottering Lycian tomb on Uzun Çarşı, but these are incidental to the joy of browsing the shops and sampling the cafés.

Beaches are little better than at Kalkan, so boat excursions are popular, including to the Greek island of **Kastellórizo** (**Meis** in Turkish) immediately opposite. The top domestic destination is the **Kekova** region, where you can peer at submerged ruins on the north shore of Kekova islet, explore the picturesque tombs of ancient Teimiussa and Simena, or climb the Crusader castle at the gulf-side village of Kale. Trips also leave from Üçağız, also on the Kekova shore, and Çayağzı near Demre.

Demre (Myra)

Demre, 35km (21 miles) east of Kaş, is a busy farming town adjacent to ancient Myra, where tourism seems to be an afterthought, with just two sights to detain you. The first is the **Church of St Nicholas** (Noël Baba Kilesisi in Turkish; daily summer 9am–7pm, winter 8.30am–5.30pm; charge), originally built during St Nicholas's tenure as local bishop *(see page 66)*. The saint's body was stolen by Italian traders in 1087 and is now in the Basilica of San Nicola in Bari, Italy. The church was extensively rebuilt by by Tsar Nicholas I of Russia in 1862 and modified more recently by Turkish archaeologists, but fresco traces remain, and the place is a major centre of pilgrimage for Russians.

About 1km (½ mile) inland are the remains of ancient **Myra** (daily 8.30am–7.30pm in summer, closes 5pm in winter; charge), with a fine theatre where many relief masks adorn toppled bits of the stage, and numerous magnificent house tombs, some still preserving faint traces of their original paint. Nearby, Hadrian built a huge granary next to Myra's harbour at **Andriake**, just inland from the modern port (and beach) of Çayağzı. There is a superior beach nearby at **Sülüklü**.

Finike and Arykanda

From Demre, the road rounds the coast to **Finike**, 30km (18 miles) east – another agricultural supply town whose tourism is largely confined to its excellent marina, a popular start- or end-point to coastal *gulet* cruises. Of the two nearby ancient sites, Limyra and **Arykanda**, the latter – 34km (21 miles) miles north along Highway 635 – is far more worthwhile. Its ruins (24hr; charge if warden present) enjoy a setting justifiably compared to Delphi in Greece, overlooking a deep valley between two high mountain ranges. Close to the car park, a basilica has fine mosaic floors, while nearby an impressive baths complex stands 10 metres (33ft) high at the façade. Further uphill are monumental tombs, an appealing theatre and attractive stadium sheltering under pines.

Olympos Beach

Olympos and Çıralı

From Finike, Highway 400 continues around the southeasternmost shoreline of Lycia 30km (19 miles) to the first turning down to the hamlet of **Olympos**, the closest spot the Turkish coast has to a backpacker hangout. Totally unlike any other local resort, this hidden valley is lined with a half-dozen so-called 'treehouse' lodges, beloved in particular of antipodeans in the weeks before and after Anzac Day at Gallipoli.

41 ▶ At the seaward end of the valley, **ancient Olympos** (daily summer 8am–7pm, winter 9am–5.30pm; charge) was an important city in the Lycian Federation, but was taken over by pirates during the 1st century BC, freed by Pompey in 67 BC and later joined to the Roman Empire. The peaceful ruins straddling a stream are only partially excavated and well overgrown, but the diligent will find an aqueduct, villa, arcaded warehouse, a monumental doorframe and – emerging at the bay – inscribed tombs with Byzantine-Genoese fortifications just above.

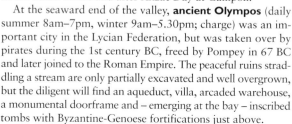

The next side-road from Highway 400 descends to the more 'adult' resort of **Çıralı**, though still with a slightly 'alternative' ethos and a superb long beach protected from overdevelopment by the forestry service – and its role as yet another turtle-nesting site. Many pansiyons and even a few discreet hotels sit a respectful distance inland, amongst citrus orchards. Still further inland and uphill at **Ulupınar** are a cluster of trout farms with attached restaurants; choose carefully, as some have become used to easy pickings from coach-tour groups.

From Çıralı, an uphill walk (or tractor-bus-ride) leads to the **Chimaera** (24hr; charge), an extraordinary natural phenomenon, best seen at dusk, in which flames, fed by methane-rich gases, issue from rock fissures. It is named after a mythical fire-breathing monster reputed to have had the head of a lion, the torso of a goat and the tail of a serpent, which was slain by local hero Bellerophon riding the winged horse Pegasus as a task set to attone for his supposed rape of the King of Xanthos' daughter. The place understandably

Olympos Teleferik

The mountains above Çıralı are part of the Beydağları National Park, their entire length threaded by the Lycian Way. An easier way to see the mountains is via the 2006-inaugurated Olympos Teleferik (www.tahtali.com; daily half-hourly 9am–7pm in summer; 10am–5pm in winter; charge), the longest cable-car ride in Europe at 4,350m (13,500ft), and the second-longest in the world. From the base station near the Phaselis turn-off, 736m (2,415ft) above sea level, it takes nearly 10 minutes to power its way up to the summit of Mt Tahtalı (the ancient Mt Olympos) at 2,365m (7,759ft), its distinctive cone-shape so pointed that the top had to be flattened to make space for the cable station, viewing deck and restaurant. The 360° views from the top are superlative.

became a shrine to Hephaestos (Vulcan), the god of fire, and also for Mithraism, an important Roman mystery religion of Indo-European origins, The flames also served as a natural lighthouse for ancient mariners.

Phaselis

About 20km (12 miles) north of the Çıralı turning, the highway reaches the access road down to **Phaselis** (daily summer 8.30am–7pm in summer, 9am–5.30pm in winter; charge). With its perfect mix of ancient ruins, sheltered beaches and shady pine forests, this makes a great day-trip, and *gulets* arrive by the score in the morning disgorging trippers. A 7th-century BC colony of Rhodes, the city prospered despite (or because of) a reputation for sycophancy and obsequiousness when met with superior force, exporting timber, rose oil and perfumes, and providing a base for pirates. There are three harbours: the fortified, exposed north harbour; the central harbour for military and small trading vessels; and the south harbour where larger vessels docked, today with the longest, sandiest beach. The main paved avenue, flanked by houses, baths a small theatre and one of the longest known Roman aqueducts, links the middle and south ports.

Phaselis beach

PAMPHYLIA

Antalya marks the transition between the wild beauty of the Lycian coast and the tamer plains of ancient Pamphylia. The landscape was not always like this – only in Byzantine times did earthquakes and silt push the coastline away from the mountains and silt up the harbours of the ancient cities. Results include a wide coastal plain with plentiful land for intensive agriculture, development and, from the tourist's point of view, lovely long sandy beaches that are ideal for paddling but scenically dull.

The Fluted Minaret (Yivli Minare)

Antalya

Described by Turkish poet Mehmet Emin Yurdakul as 'a charming girl watching her beautiful visage in the clear mirror of the Mediterranean', **Antalya** has elicited paeans of praise from visitors across the centuries – including Ibn Battuta and Freya Stark. According to legend, 2nd-century BC King Attalos II of Pergamon chose the spot for the city because it was 'heaven on earth'. These days, Antalya is a huge city, the eighth largest in Turkey with a population of just over one million and getting bigger all the time. But with its broad bay, backed by the seasonally snow-capped Toros Mountains, and the lozenge-shaped central harbour surrounded by the walled old town, Kaleiçi, it is still incredibly beautiful. It also has a good collection of boutique hotels,

43

Fine facilities

'There are eight bath-houses in the city, most within the walls, and a bazaar on the outskirts. Here there are twenty Muslim neighbourhoods and four Greek neighbourhoods, but the non-Muslims know no Greek. The harbour has space for two hundred ships, but since wind and gales are frequent in the harbour, the ships moor to high rocks on the shore.'

The renowned Turkish traveller Evliya Celebi, who visited Antalya in 1671–2.

excellent restaurants, sophisticated clubs and bars, and excellent shopping.

The town's closest beach lies to the west in modern **Konyaaltı** district, backed by hotels, restaurants, parks and entertainment venues. This is also the home of the **Antalya Müzesi** (2km (1 mile) west of the town centre; Tue–Sun summer 9am–7.30pm, winter 8.30am–4.30pm; charge), a truly world-class museum, with many of the statues and mosaics from Perge, Aspendos and Xanthos, as well as early prehistoric items found locally, a superb selection of decorative sarcophagi, and ethnographic collections covering everything from carpets to traditional dress and carriages. Look out for the silver reliquary that once held the bones of St Nicholas.

The city's other sites are all within the walls of **Kaleiçi**, entered through **Hadrian's Gate**, a triumphal arch built when the emperor visited in AD130. Nearby are the **Saat Kulesi** (clocktower) built in 1244 (although the clock was added much later), 16th-century **Mehmet Paşa Camii** and the distinctive **Yivli Minare** (Fluted Minaret), with its decorative turquoise and blue tiles, whose adjoining mosque is now an art gallery. Write a wish and put the paper in the ancient olive tree next to the minaret and it will come true. Further along, the **Kesik Minare** (Broken Minaret) is an all-purpose religious site that has, in its time, been a Roman temple, a Byzantine church and an Ottoman mosque. On the headland overlooking the harbour, the squat round **Hıdırlık Kulesi** may have begun life as a lighthouse in the 2nd century AD. The only museum in Kaleiçi is the **Mediterranean Civilisations and Research Institute** (**Suna-İnan Kıraç Akdeniz Araştırma Enstitütü**; Kocatepe Sok 25; Thur–Tue summer 9am–noon & 2–7.30pm, winter 9am–noon, 1–6pm; charge), a small, private museum occupying two restored Ottoman mansions and the Orthdox church of **Agios Georgios**. The church contains Çanakkale ceramics, the houses rich archives and rooms restored as tableaux. Antalya's oldest **hamam** (bath-house) is just opposite. All around are a maze of small steep streets and alleys filled with old Ottoman houses, many restored as accommodation, restaurants and shops that make this an ideal place to stroll, stopping for an occasional glass of black tea and some hard bargaining. Boat trips leave from the old harbour.

Hadrian's Gate

Termessos and Karain Mağarası

Termessos amphitheatre

From the car park, it takes a good 25 minutes to ascend to the romantically unexcavated ruins of **Termessos** **44** (37km/22 miles northwest of Antalya; daily summer 9am–7.30pm, winter 8.30am–5pm; charge) which teeter precariously under the rugged crags of Güllük Dağı. Even Alexander the Great gave up on the climb as its notoriously warlike and freedom-loving citizens hurled boulders over the ramparts at his troops. For those who make the trek, the setting is incomparable, with the theatre sandwiched between a cliff and a deep gorge. Termessos also has a large gymnasium, odeon, Zeus temple, cisterns and a necropolis. The surrounding Güllük Dağı National Park is surpassingly beautiful, its conifer forests home to wild goats and fallow deer.

The Toros (Taurus) Mountains are riddled with caves, many bearing evidence of human and proto-human habitation going back millennia, as well as fine stalactite and stalagmite formations. Some are open to the public, others can be visited by expert cavers. The first people started living in **45** ▶ **Karain Mağarası** (Karain Cave; 27km/17 miles northwest of Antalya, off Highway 650 to Burdur; 6km/4 miles from the main road; daily 8.30am–5pm; charge) about 30,000 years ago, and habitation continued for another 20,000 years, producing an invaluable stream of prehistoric evidence. It is easy to visit, with stairs, lights and a small site museum.

Perge and Belek

As you leave Antalya and head east, the main road is lined by outlet malls, discount stores and huge emporia selling everything from gold and diamonds to carpets.

The **Kurşunlu Şelale** (Kurşunlu Falls; 23km/14 miles east of Antalya, 7km/4miles off main road; daily 8.30am– 5.30pm; charge) is a popular daytrip for families from Antalya, with a picnic area and walks surrounding high, stepped waterfalls.

A few kilometres further on, **Perge** (Perga in Greek; daily 9am–7.30pm in summer, until 6pm in winter; charge and parking fees) is one of the most extensive and best preserved of Turkey's ancient cities. Founded by some time after 1100BC, it was used by Alexander the Great during his Pamphylian campaign, eventually passing to Pergamon and finally expiring late in the Byzantine era when its harbour silted up. The impressive monuments begin on the drive towards the main site with the 14,000-seat theatre (closed for works) and a superbly preserved 12,000-seat stadium (both 2nd century AD). The entrance was through the giant red 3rd-century BC Hellenistic gates from where visitors could turn left towards a series of elegant and highly sophisticated baths, right towards the 4th-century AD forum or continue straight along the colonnad-

Kurşunlu Şelale

ed main street, its marble paving stones still clearly showing the ruts of carts and carriages, many of the shops to either side still with mosaic floors. At the far end, on the acropolis, are fragmentary remains of the earliest city. Perge is one of the start-points for the **St Paul Trail** *(see page 92)*.

Until the early 1980s, the long stretch of flat sand beach between Perge and Aspendos was virgin territory. Now there **48** is a whole town, **Belek**, complete with shopping malls, a long line of luxury hotels, a great many apartment blocks and – the focus for all this frenetic building – 16 world-class championship **golf courses**, with more planned. Many people who stay here never get further than the golf links, but most of the hotels lay on a variety of other activities. Belek is within easy reach of Antalya and the local sights, the beaches are superb (a view shared by local loggerhead turtles, *see page 56*), and it's affordable.

The theatre at Aspendos

Aspendos and Köprülü Kanyon

Aspendos (31km/19 miles east of Perge, plus 5km/3 miles more from main road; daily 9am–7.30pm in summer, 8.30am–5pm in winter; charge) was probably founded at about the same time as Perge. Although now several kilometres inland, it was a port, specialising in luxuries and staples such as salt, oil, wine and horses, and once it became the property of Pergamon, its wealth and status

Rafting the Köprülü Kanyon

were assured. But while there are various remains here, few visitors notice them, choosing to concentrate solely on the fabulous 15,000-seat theatre, built by the architect Zeno during the reign of Emperor Marcus Aurelius (AD161–80), and probably the finest surviving Roman theatre in the world. It seats up to 15,000, with 40 rows of marble seats divided by 10 staircases in the lower section and 21 above. A richly decorated stage wall once held marble statues, most of which are now in Antalya Museum. It is still used for an annual June festival of ballet and opera *(see page 99)* as well as other events. Elsewhere, look out for the elegant 880m (2,888ft) stretch of aqueduct (1st century AD) and the beautiful 13th-century Selçuk stone bridge across the Köprüçay.

Just after Aspendos, a road turns off inland climbing into the foothills along the Köprü river valley. After about 43km (28 miles) a cluster of little restaurants marks the beginning of the **Köprülü Kanyon**, a stunning chasm that offers some of the country's most famous (and most crowded) whitewater rafting, great wild trout for fishermen and gourmets and lovely walks in the fresh mountain air. A single-arched Roman stone bridge crosses the gorge and a gravel road uses it, climbing ever higher to the village of **Altınkaya** (Zerk) where the ruins of ancient **Selge**, once a city of 20,000 people, are threaded amongst back-garden cabbages and fruit trees in a spectacular setting.

Side and Alarahan

Pronounced 'See-day' and meaning pomegranate (a symbol of fertility) in a lost Anatolian language, **Side**, 38km (24 miles) southeast of Aspendos, has been a holiday resort since Anthony and Cleopatra met up here, supposedly to negotiate a timber concession. Then it combined hedonistic pursuits with piracy and slaving; these days, it concentrates on the former. The ancient monuments are threaded through the modern resort, which is delightful out of season and, while

Dining out in Side

tamer than it once was, can still be a heaving mass of alcohol-fuelled bodies in summer. Resort hotels fan out along the beaches to either side of the core old village on its promontory. At the entrance to the town centre are the freestanding, 20,000-seat **theatre** and the **Archaeological Museum** (Tue–Sun summer 9am–noon, 1.30–7.30pm, winter closes

Alarahan fortress

5.30pm; charge) housed in the former Roman baths. Beside the former harbour, perfectly positioned to catch the sunset, are the **Temples of Athena and Apollo**.

Manavgat is Side's much larger neighbour, with little to recommend it to tourists other than boat trips to the local waterfalls. At **Alarahan** (35km/22 miles east of Side, 9km/6 miles off the main road; daily 9am–11pm) is one of the finest of some 200 Seljuk *kervansaray*, built in about 1231 by Seljuk Sultan Alâeddin Keykubad I for those travelling the Silk Road between Konya and Alanya. Set a day's journey apart, these institutions offered lodging to travellers and their animals, along with medical assistance and spiritual guidance. Today, the interior is full of souvenir stalls, with one hall set aside for entertaining tour groups with dinner and belly-dancing. An impressive Byzantine-Seljuk **fortress**, reached by a steep 15-minute walk, garlands the mountain just north of the *kervanseray*.

Alanya

Alanya, 39km (24 miles) east of Alarahan, was until the millennium an almost entirely German domain, although the Brits and Russians are now invading in search of cheaper

Damlataş Mağarası

property prices and huge sandy beaches. With its own international airport 40km (X miles) away at Gazipa, finally operational in 2011, further exponential growth around this resort is assured.

Alanya is not particularly attractive, with ranks of mass market hotels and apartment blocks both in town and stretching out along the beaches. **İncekum**, 20km (12 miles) west, is the place to come if reasonably priced sun, sand and party-ing is your thing. However, it does also have some history, with a fortress built by a 1st-century BC pirate chief, Diodotus Tryphon, before he was kicked out of the region by Pompey; Coracesium, as Alanya was then known, soon joined the Roman Empire. In 44BC, Mark Anthony gave the whole region to Cleopatra. The city became Kalonoros under the Byzantines and was then renamed again by Seljuk Sultan Alâeddin Keykubad I in 1221 when he made the town his summer capital.

Near the harbour the 35m (115ft) **Kızıl Kule** (Red Tower) was built in 1226 by a Syrian architect for Sultan Alâeddin Keykubad I to protect the dockyard. Inside it has five storeys, with arched galleries surrounding a huge water cistern. The tower now houses a small ethnographic museum (Tue–Sun 8am–noon, 1.30–5pm; charge). The main **Alanya Museum** (Azaklar Sokağı; Tue–Sun 8.30am–noon, 1.30–5.30pm; charge) is small but well-displayed, with a mix of archaeo-logical and ethnographic displays.

Nearby, **Damlataş Mağarası** (Weeping Cave; 10am–7pm; charge) has two chambers with great stalactite and stalagmite formations, high humidity and elevated levels of carbon dioxide, natural ionisation and radiation that make it a supposedly great cure for asthma and rheumatism (if you sit in the cave daily 6–10am for 21 days).

Boat trips round the harbour are the only way to see the **Tersane**, the last remaining Seljuk dockyard in Turkey, dating from 1227. Positioned right on the water, it consists of a row of five huge open workshops with arched roofs. The trips also offer spectacular views of various sea-caves and the **Citadel** (daily summer 9am–7.30pm, winter 8.30am– 5pm; charge), built onto a soaring 250m (820ft) seacliff and surrounded by vast defensive walls with 150 bastions and 400 water cisterns. If you want to go up, there are 4km (2½ miles) of hairpin bends to climb, or alternatively a bus service.

Alanya Harbour

WHAT TO DO

SHOPPING

Turkey is one of the world's great bazaars, and bridging Europe and Asia, it has much of the best of both for sale – along with an awful lot of tat, both domestic and imported. Shopping in Turkey is an art form, and an entertainment. Get into the mood, and remember that however persuasive someone is and however much of their tea you have drunk, you do not have to buy. The Turks are happy to negotiate in all major currencies, with significant discounts for paying with cash rather than plastic. On major purchases look out for shops displaying a tax refund sticker and you may be able to reclaim the VAT. Any antiquities need a clearance certificate for export.

Shopping habits are changing. There are far more fixed price stores, and out-of-town malls, supermarkets and factory discount outlets have emerged. But the most fun is still to be had in the central bazaars, of which the best on the coast are in İzmir, Bodrum and Marmaris and, for purely photographic purposes, the weekly markets where local farmers descend with their colourful heaps of tomatoes, aubergines and watermelons.

What to Buy

Carpets. Turkey is the original home of the knotted pile carpet, introduced by the Seljuks in the 12th century. There is a huge array of styles, techniques and designs, from thick, shaggy Çanakkale carpets to the soft colours and geometric motifs of Milaş near Bodrum or the earthy geometric designs of Döşemealtı near Antalya. Finest of all are the intricate flo-

Reflections in Bodrum harbour

ral patterns and smooth silks of Hereke carpets. Also look out for kilims (flat-weave rugs) which have been produced here since at least the first millennium BC, *cicims* which have designs like embroidery stitched into them, and *sumaks*, kilims from the far east with an overlay of figurative stitching.

Take time to look around and gauge prices before committing yourself; perhaps also have a look at one of the state-run fixed price shops or weavers' cooperatives which also give demonstrations of carpet-making, and at any ethnographic museum's carpet/*kilim* section.

Fashion. Turkey's textile industry is huge and many of the world's top designers manufacture their clothes here. The result is an excellent three-tier shopping market – real designer gear in chic Bodrum, Antalya and İzmir boutiques, end-of-series or seconds designer gear in outlet malls outside the major towns, and a thriving – if highly illegal – trade in variable-quality fakes. Off the designer treadmill, look at the

How to Buy a Carpet

A good Turkish carpet is an expensive purchase and buying can be a minefield – are the materials and dyes natural or synthetic, how many knots per unit area are there, is it actually old or has it been aged with the help of bleach or strong sunlight? The rule of thumb is that natural is best, with silk best of all, then wool, then blends of silk/cotton, wool/cotton. Dyes are preferably natural, although many of the newer synthetics are much subtler than the old garish ones. Traditionally, every village had its own designs and every design told a story. These days more carpets are made to suit foreign tastes and the old traditions are vanishing. If you buy a genuine antique, you will need an export certificate from the relevant authority; the dealer should be able to arrange it for you. Most dealers will also arrange postage, but take it with you if at all possible and benefit from your country's accompanied-goods customs allowance.

Carpets from Milaş

silk scarves and pashminas, thick, cuddly cotton bathrobes (with towelling to match) or made-to-measure clothes from a tailor in the bazaar.

Leather. The leather market is overwhelmed by fake designer bags (some of excellent quality), but Turkey produces fine leather goods at surprisingly reasonable prices. If you want a new bag, belt, wallet, jacket, or even sandals this is definitely the place to shop. Many shops also offer a custom-design 'made-to-measure' service, offering you the coat of your dreams delivered to your hotel. Check quality and price as both can vary hugely.

Other Great Buys. Jewellery can be a steal with delicate filigree and pieces custom-made to your specifications in the big warehouses near the major archaeological sites; gold and silver are sold by weight, with only a small premium for workmanship. Ceramics follow traditional patterns from the famous İznik tiles – the tiles themselves have made a come-

Blue beads

Ubiquitous blue glass beads (*nazar boncuğu*) are traditional amulets designed to ward off the evil eye. Any bad luck is directed into the beads which will break once their work is done.

back, and are very popular with Turkish householders. Antique shops are full of lovely old copper-ware, though it's getting scarcer and is thus steeply priced. For 'little presents', good options are *lokum* (Turkish delight), herbal teas, pine nuts, olive oil, soap and spices; inlaid chess sets and backgammon boards; shadow-puppets; meerschaum pipes; hubble-bubbles; slippers; and of course blue beads to ward off the evil eye.

ENTERTAINMENT

There is plenty of evening entertainment all along the coast, starting inside the resort hotels, which lay on extravagant cabaret-shows, belly-dance evenings, casinos, and pulsating nightclubs for their guests. Most also open to non-residents. Beyond the hotels, town streets are lined with bars, while most resorts host a collection of noisy dance clubs and old-fashioned discos, some of which have achieved international fame. However, almost all after-dark activity takes place only in season (late May/early June to late September). Otherwise, much of the coast is ghostly quiet, the domain of a few locally patronized restaurants and perhaps one or two low-key bars.

The exceptions to the rule are İzmir and Antalya, both proper cities with a full local cultural programme, including resident symphony orchestras. Both have film festivals, while Aspendos near Antalya also hosts a ballet and opera festival in the magnificent Roman theatre *(see page 79)*. But if you really want to be Turkish for an evening, search out a backstreet *türkü bar*, where you can hear mildly electrified versions of traditional Turkish folksongs.

Bars and Clubs

Kuşadası, Bodrum and Marmaris all have designated 'Bar/ Pub Lanes' or variations thereon, though usually the best clubs are off this strip, and there are persistent reports at Kuşadası and Marmaris of drink-spiking on these lanes. İzmir's nightlife is centred amongst the old houses of Pounda (Alsancak) district. Eski Foça has just a cluster of musical bars in the old market, Çeşme even less, and Kalkan much the same. Fethiye is noted for its old-town *türkü* bars, while Kaş has one of the most congenial ranges of nightspots on the entire coast.

In Bodrum, **Halikarnas** (Cumhuriyet Caddesi 178, www. halikarnas.com.tr) is a long-established, internationally renowned (and expensive) open-air club with huge crowds after its midnight laser show. **Hadigari** (Dr Alim Bey Caddesi 37, www.hadigari.com.tr), the oldest bar here, hosts live

Halikarnas in Bodrum

concerts in alternation with DJ party nights. In Marmaris, **Crazy Daisy** (www.crazydaisybar.com) is the doyenne of the Bar Lane outfits, with eardrum-shattering music and a capacity of 1,300. Kaş can offer durable **Red Point Bar** (Süleyman Topçu Sokağı), a converted barn with dance-floor, and a lovely sit-down spot in **Hideway** (Cumhuriyet Cad 16, lane off old market square), with a retro rock-and-blues soundtrack. Standouts among Antalya's very scattered venues include **Club Ally** (http://ally.teknotalya.com), the biggest in the old town with seven bars, and **Club Arma** near the old harbour (tel: 0242-244 9710, www.clubarma.com.tr), a chic open-air spot adjoining a fancy seafood restaurant, installed in an old Italian-built industrial installation.

ACTIVE PURSUITS

Most larger hotels have gyms and pools; many have tennis courts. The biggest run regular classes in everything from martial arts and aerobics to yoga. Belek, near Antalya *(see page 78)*, was purpose-built as a world-class golfing centre with 16 championship courses.

Sailing and Yachting
Yachting is increasingly popular, with sleek marinas in many resorts; the tourist office can give you details of facilities and fees. Currents and winds along the coasts can be strong.

One of the best ways of seeing the coast between Bodrum and Finike is on a so-called 'Blue Cruise'. The traditional wooden **gulets** used sleep between six and 30 and come fully staffed. Fairly standard itineraries are offered, anchoring in small bays and off islands to snorkel and sunbathe in deserted coves, arriving at coastal archaeological sites by boat and dropping into the main resorts for some shopping therapy and a restaurant meal. Arrange such cruises either through

Banana boat fun on the Kalkan coast

local operators in most resorts (especially Bodrum, Fethiye or Marmaris) or through specialists like Cavurali (tel: Turkey, 0242-419 2441; www.cavurali.com), Day Dreams (tel: UK 01884-849200, www.turkishcruises.co.uk), or SCIC (tel: UK 020-8510 9292, www.tussockcruising.com).

Watersports

On this hugely long coast, there is every possibility for messing about on, in, above or below the water. The largest resort hotels have their own watersports facilities, the rest all have links with nearby outfitters. The main **windsurfing/ kitesurfing** centres are Gökçeada, the Çeşme peninsula, and the Bodrum peninsula; the best **scuba-diving** is off Ayvalık, Bodrum, Kalkan and Kaş. Various areas are closed to diving because of military restrictions or the presence of underwater antiquities, so it's advisable to always go under the aegis of a local scuba outfitter.

Divers' delights

Divers can find plenty to entertain them, from marble columns deposited by ancient earthquakes, to Roman amphorae and a wide variety of sealife. This ranges from moray eels and loggerhead turtles to groupers, cardinal fish, flying fish, skates, barracuda, rainbow wrasse, damselfish, bonita, garfish, amberjack, various breams, octopus, and dolphins.

Inland, the Dalaman Çayı, the Eşen Çayı and the Köprülü Kanyon offer opportunities for **canoeing** or **whitewater rafting**, while **sea-kayaking** is increasingly popular. The foothills inland from Kaş are the main venue for **canyoning**.

Other Activities

Hot air ballooning is sporadically offered in the Antalya area, with trips over the Köprülü Kanyon and Aspendos; **paragliding** is a more reliable feature at Ölüdeniz, launching from 1,975m (6,480ft) high Mt Baba Daği overhead. **Jeep safaris**, **horse-riding**, **canyoning** and **rock-climbing** can be arranged at almost every resort from Marmaris to Kaş.

There are two particularly fine marked and documented **hiking** routes: the Lycian Way, which dips and climbs through the mountains along the Mediterranean coast from Ölüdeniz to Antalya; and the St Paul Trail from Perge to Yalvaç, northeast of Lake Eğirdir, with a second branch starting at Aspendos, 40km (25 miles) east of Antalya and joining the first route at the Roman site of Adada. Each takes about a month to complete in entirety (though many people only do the best bits). Both trails are covered on www.lycianway.com, through which the official map-guides can be ordered.

Less energetically, there are rich **birdwatching** areas behind Belek (see page 78); in the Köyceğiz reedbeds, near Dalyan (see page 57); and at the Çiğli-Sasallı coastal bird sanctuary northwest of İzmir, which records up to 250 species per year, some resident, some migratory.

Activity Outfitters

Alternatif Outdoor, Çamlık Sok 10/1, Marmaris, tel: 0252-417 2720, www.alternatifraft.com. Specialist outfitters for sea-kayaking, rafting, canyoning and the like in southwestern Turkey, with a good service record.

BT Adventure and Diving, İbrahim Serin Caddes 10, Kaş, tel: 0242-836 3737, www.bt-turkey.com. Well established outfit, offering diving, canyoning, sea-kayaking at Kekova, and mountain-biking; complete packages using their two hotels.

Gökçeada Windsurf Club, Aydıncık, Gökçeada (İmroz), tel: 0286-898 1016, www.surfgokceada.com. At the island's most beautiful beach, this windsurfing school also offers complete packages at its comfortable adjacent hotel.

Kalkan Diving/Aquasports, Kalamar Beach Club, Kalkan, tel: 0532-553 2006, www.kalkandiving.com. The best surviving operator here, offering dives and courses at all levels

Young sailing cadets at Marmaris

Shooting the rapids in the Köprülü Kanyon

around Kalkan bay's islands, reefs and walls.

Kite Turkey, Alaçatı, tel: 0538-381 5686. Kite-surfing in ideal conditions at Alaçatı and Urla on the Çeşme peninusla, plus Gökova, near Marmaris.

Körfez Diving, Central quay, Ayvalık, tel: 0266-312 499, www.korfezdiving.com. One of a handful of scuba operators taking advantage of the deep-water red coral, submerged antiquities and caves in the area.

Medraft, Yeşilbahçe Mahallesi, Portakal Çiçeği Bulvarı, Hüseyin Kuzu Ap.14/3, Antalya, tel: 0242-312 5770, www.medraft.com.tr. Whitewater rafting in the Köprülü Kanyon; jeep safaris; cycling; and hiking, much of this from their own lodge near Zerk village.

Patara Canoeing, Gelemiş village, tel: 0242-843 5034, www.pataracanoeing.com. Half-day paddling tours on the gentle Eşen Çayı from Xanthos to the beach, suitable for all ages.

Rush Windsurfing, Bitez Beach, Bodrum Peninsula tel: www.rushwindsurf.itgo.com. Reputable, long-running school which can arrange all-in windsurfing holidays locally.

Trooper Tours, Tayahatun Sok, Sukran Han 3, Sirkeci, İstanbul, tel: 0212-520 0434, www.troopertours.com. Specialist day and weekend tours to Gallipoli from İstanbul.

Spectator Sports

Turkey is football mad, with every major town fielding a team. The country's four first-division side are mostly in İstanbul, but there are plenty of matches to catch elsewhere. There are also a number of more esoteric spectator sports such as oil-wrestling (with the competitors greased up with olive oil), mainly near Edirne in Thrace, although there are matches elsewhere; camel-wrestling, a winter feature of İzmir and Aydın; and *cirit*, traditional jousting on horseback from eastern Turkey.

BATHS AND SPAS

Forget your soothing whalesong, scented lotions and dim lights – a **hamam** (Turkish bath) is a much more robust experience, designed to get you clean. It is a slice of history, the direct descendant of the Roman bath.

It is also totally invigorating, and is a completely traditional Turkish experience. Many multi-star hotels have their own hamams but most larger towns also have traditional baths that have been operating for hundreds of years, and cost a fraction of the price.

Bathers at Pamukkale

If you want the whalesong and designer sundries, however, there is plenty of that available as well. Most of the five-star hotels and certain smaller boutique hotels have spas, while some – such as the Six Senses Spa at the Kempinski Barbaros Bay in Bodrum *(see page 138)* – are world-class destinations.

With a considerable amount of geothermal activity rumbling away beneath its surface, Turkey also has numerous mineral-rich **hot springs**, **mud pools** and **therapeutic caves**; alongside these, full-on **health spas** or even medically approved therapy centres are beginning to appear. There are several concentrations along the coast – at Gönen near Çanakkale, at Balçova and Ilıca on the Çeşme peninsula, at Lake Köyceğiz near Dalyan, and inland at Pamukkale.

Agamemnon Thermal Spa and Wellness Centre, Hüseyin Öğütçen Caddesi 2, Balçova, İzmir, tel: 0232-259 0102. Standing on the site of the Baths of Agamemnon, supposedly used by the Greek commander for treating soldiers wounded at the siege of Troy, this is the flagship of the medical spas, with a huge capacity.

Bodrum Hamamı, Cevat Sakir Caddesi, Fabrika Sok 42, Bodrum, tel: 0252-313 4129, www.bodrumhamami.com.tr. Daily 6am–midnight. A traditional hamam, beautifully restored with stone cladding. Single-sex facilities.

How to Have a Turkish Bath

Your Turkish bath starts in the reception area (*camekân*) where you are given a locker, a sarong (*peştamal*), a towel and wooden clogs (*takunya*). You can keep your underwear on or go nude beneath the sarong – whichever makes you feel comfortable. Most baths are separated by sex, although a very few in tourist areas offer mixed bathing. You then go through to the domed main hot room (*hararet*), with a large marble slab (*göbek taşı*) surrounded by small alcoves (*halvet*) with taps of hot and cold water. Wash yourself down and stretch out on the slab to steam and get scrubbed down. This involves a rough exfoliating goat-hair or loofah-fibre glove (*kese*), large quantities of soap suds and buckets of water. A full body oil massage is usually an optional extra before you relax under your towel with a hot or cold drink.

Old Turkish Bath, Hamam Sokak 2, Paspatur Bazaar, Fethiye, tel: 0252-614 9318, www.oldturkishbath.com. Daily 7am–midnight. Both men-only and mixed facilities are available at this 16th-century hamam in the bazaar area.

Spa Hotel Therme Maris, Incebel Mevkii 48770 Dalaman, tel: 0252-694 8334, www.thermemaris.com. Not a great location (next to the runway of Dalaman airport) but this is a serious spa resort with mud pools, thermal springs, and medical staff on site.

Enjoying the mud pools in Dalyan

Sultaniye Natural Hot Springs and Ilıca Mud Baths, Köyceğiz Lakeshore and Dalyan Çayı, Dalyan. The mud baths are open 24hrs but tend to get crowded at mid-day. The best part of the Sultaniye complex is the domed, round pool dating back to ancient times.

CHILDREN'S TURKISH COAST

Turkey is a great place to take children on holiday, although it is probably sensible to avoid the heat of high summer if possible. Make sure you take hats and high-factor sunblock, and provide lots of liquids. The country is very child-friendly, with good medical facilities. Most infant supplies are freely available in supermarkets and pharmacies, although you may want to take your tried and tested brands of bottled baby food and formula with you. Food for older kids is relatively simple, healthy and delicious – made-to-order will be more hygienic – and it's easy to persuade children to eat things such as *köfte* (mini hamburgers) and chips.

For those with younger children, many hotels have kids' clubs and baby-sitting services. If you want a gently shelving, sandy beach, it is probably better to look on the Aegean Coast or between Antalya and Alanya (although Dalyan and Patara also have suitable beaches). For older children looking for watersports, hiking and sightseeing, consider the wilder Lycian Coast between Fethiye and Antalya.

Beyond the kids' club and the beach, there's a whole world of excitement, from caves such as the Karain Cave near Antalya *(see page 76)*, to horse-riding at several resorts, canoeing on the gentle Eşen Çayı and scrambling across the ruins of ancient cities.

Kids in the Saklıkent Gorge

There are also **waterparks** of various shapes and sizes, headed by the vast Adaland in Kuşadası (tel: 0256-618 1252, www.adaland.com); this is the largest waterpark in Europe, with rides, a seapark and a dolphinarium. Antalya's giant BeachPark at Konyaaltı (tel: 0242-249 0900, www.beachpark.com.tr) includes an Aqualand and a DolphinLand offering the opportunity to swim with dolphins. There are smaller parks in Marmaris, Fethiye and Alanya.

Festivals and Seasonal Events

January *Selçuk*: Camel Wrestling Festival, 3rd Sunday.

February *İzmir*: camel wrestling.

March *İzmir*: European Jazz Days.

April *Gallipoli*: 25 April ceremonies for Anzac Day, in memory of the Australian and New Zealand troops who died here.

May *Ephesus*: Festival in the ancient theatre; *Marmaris*: International Yachting Week; *Alanya*: Beach Volley Championships.

June *Aspendos:* Opera and Ballet Festival; *İzmir* (*Ephesus* and *Çeşme* too): International Music Festival; *Kaş*: Lycia Culture and Art Festival.

July *Çeşme*: Çeşme International Song Contest; *Antalya and Aspendos*: International Folk Festival.

September *Antalya*: International Akdeniz Song Contest; *Bodrum*: Ballet & Opera Festival around the castle; *Marmaris*: Marmaris Tango Festival.

October *Antalya*: Altın Portakal (Golden Orange) Film Festival – increasingly prestigious forum for international and local directors; *Bodrum*: International Bodrum Cup – yacht race with special provision for traditional wood-hulled vessels.

November *Alanya*: International Triathlon Competition (swimming, cycling and running); *Marmaris*: International Yacht Race – Turkey's last sailing competition of the season; nationwide, 10 November: anniversary of the death of Atatürk.

December *Demre*: Special Mass on 6 December honouring Saint Nicholas of Myra, aka Santa Claus.

Turkey also celebrates several moveable Muslim festivals each year, chief amongst them the month-long, dawn-to-dust fast of **Ramazan**. Tourist restaurants remain open for lunch but be discreet about eating and drinking or smoking in public. Dusk signals the start of a huge meal. The end of Ramazan is celebrated by the three-day Şeker Bayramı (Sugar Festival). This is followed about ten weeks later by the five-day Kurban Bayramı (Feast of the Sacrifice).

EATING OUT

Turkey lays claim to creating one of the world's four great cuisines (along with France, Italy and China), so any visit should involve sampling as many traditional dishes as possible in authentic surroundings, rather than hotel-restaurants. In season, many restaurants begin serving around noon and stay open until nearly midnight. Set meal times, and required reservations, are rare except in more upmarket eateries. A tip of around 10 percent is customary, unless there is a substantial service charge – identified as either *garsoniye* or *servis* (sometimes both).

Children are welcome in all establishments except the rowdier *meyhanes*. A ban on smoking in public places is generally enforced inside, making open-air restaurant terraces very popular. Some restaurants have separate seating areas for women and children – the *aile salonu* – but these are rare in resorts.

Hygiene and cleanliness may be pillars of Islam but some restaurants, especially in mass-market resorts, are known to cut corners, particularly with proper heating and refrigeration of foods. Especially in mid-summer, always prefer cold appetisers from the start of a batch, and avoid cooked dishes stored uncovered or at tepid temperatures.

WHERE TO EAT AND DRINK

A *lokanta* is the main type of restaurant found all over Turkey, catering to workers at lunch and, often, to neighbourhood families in the evening. The six to eight steam-tray dishes offered on a given day are displayed in a glass case, served on request; expect one or two meat or fish dishes, often prepared as stews, with vegetable and rice or potato accompaniments. Adventurous chefs are increasingly part of the *lokanta* scene, with daily specials written on a board. A full-blown *restoran*, or restaurant, may be only marginally fancier than a *lokanta*, but can also be quite elegant, with a fuller range of salads, grills and starters.

A *meyhane* (tavern) was traditionally a male-dominated establishment where food was on barely equal footing with alcohol (especially *rakı*), but more recently women are generally welcome, and the emphasis has shifted to quality dishes that go well with drink. There will often be recorded music, or on certain nights live performances of poignant old-timey songs.

A *pastahane* (or *pastane*) is a patisserie offering a mix of both oriental sweetmeats and western-style cakes and profiteroles; you can usually sit at a table and have tea or coffee, or buy to take out. A *muhallebici* is a *pastane* whose remit extends to the healthier milk-based desserts like *sütlaç* (rice pudding) *kazandibi* (upside-down chicken-breast

Waterfront restaurant at Ayvalık

Simit bread rings

pudding), *keşkül* (custard) or the divine *aşure* (so-called Noah's Pudding).

A *pideci* or *pide salonu* specialises in that made-to-order dish (see below); a few also offer some salads and side dishes, and may even be licensed. A *simithane* (bun shop), often favoured by youth, is a cheerful new trend in Turkish snack venues (a *simit* is a bagel-like ring studded with sesame-seeds, tasty with cream cheese or jam).

A *kebapcı* serves that ubiquitous staple of Turkish cuisine, the kebab; lamb is continually roasted on a revolving spit, ready to be sliced and skewered on a *şiş* with roast vegetables. *Dönercis* offer roast döner, an initially conical mass of fatty lamb or chicken which as the day progresses gets whittled down into thin slices served atop pide (pitta bread) or rice with garnish.

Büfes (roadside kiosks) sell convenience foods, snacks or tasty grilled cheese sandwich *(tost)*. Street carts sell everything from roasted chestnuts in winter to ice cream in summer, but should not be patronised for perishable dishes like *midya dolması* (rice-stuffed mussels) or anything with mayonnaise.

A *kahvehane* is a coffee-house for men, with women not welcome. Much the same can be said for the occasionally encounterd *birahane* (beerhall). Visit a *şaraphane* (wine bar), however, and you find slick service and excellent food with a comprehensive wine list and nibbles.

WHAT TO EAT

The stars of Turkish cuisine are the unfailingly delicious appetisers known as *meze*, which are a feature of *meyhanes* and better resort *lokantas*. Several *meze* platters can in fact be so satisfying that you may not need a main course. Typical choices are piping hot cheese rolls *(sigara böreği)*, smoky-flavoured aubergine purée *(patlıcan salatası)*, or assorted stuffed vegetables *(dolmalar)*. Sophisticated specialities include *çerkez tavuğı* (shredded chicken and walnuts) and *arnavut çiğer* (Albanian-style liver).

Typical vegetable accompaniments are simply prepared beans, okra, cauliflower or perhaps *turşu* (pickled vegetables); salad is typically the micro-chopped *çoban salatası* – greens like rocket or lettuce are relatively rare.

Meaty main courses rely on various cuts of lamb or chicken, doled out with garnish and rice *(pilav)*, often with chips as well; pork is not served in this Muslim country, and beef

Sweet Teeth

Syrupy pastries like *baklava* (phyllo pastry with syrup and nuts) are consumed with tea or coffee, usually mid morning or during the afternoon. But Turks also love *dondurma,* the putty-like ice cream that originated in central Anatolia and is named after the town, *Maraş Dondurması.* It includes *sahlep* (ground orchid root) which makes it, quite literally, elastic.

Turkish delight, *lokum*, was the confection creation of an İstanbul confectioner, Hacı Bekir, in the early 19th century. Highly prized by women of the harem, it is a typically Turkish gift to take home – as is the rich and gritty sesame treat, *helva*, more likely to be some variation on baked flour, butter, sugar and flavoured water than the sesame-paste concoction known in the west.

A *meze* platter

is usually ground. Clay-pot stews *(güveç)*, simmered or oven-baked, are made with vegetables and either meat or seafood. Aubergine is a staple food: grilled, stewed, stuffed and roasted or as part of a *kebap*. The Ottoman court kitchens prided themselves on having 150 recipes for this vegetable.

Fresh fish, often various kinds of farmed bream, is a mainstay of menus along the Aegean and Mediterranean coasts, where restaurants display their wares (often not local) on ice and serve it simply grilled. Always establish per-kilo or per-portion prices beforehand to avoid later misunderstandings..

Turkish **breakfast**, available at even the most modest pansiyons, typically includes sliced cucumber, olives, tomato, a hard-boiled egg, yogurt, seasonal fruit and bread slices to be topped with jam or honey. In multistar hotels, buffet breakfast can be elaborate, with omelettes live-cooked and various charcuterie laid out. Out in town, you can patronise a counter or cart from which *börek*, a fluffy cheese pastry, is served.

Later on, the most ubiquitous snack in rural areas is *gözleme*, a paratha-like delicacy cooked on a *saç* (griddle), stuffed with a variety of fillings. Other sit-down snacks include *pide* (Turkish pizza), an elongated dough 'boat' topped with cheese, minced meat, egg or other choices and baked in a wood-fired oven. *Lahmacun*, a round thin crust with a spicy meat and tomato topping, has Armenian/Arab roots. *Ayran* (diluted yogurt) is the traditional accompaniment to any of these.

Beverages

Turkey is an overwhelmingly Muslim country but most Turks have a relaxed attitude towards alcohol in coastal resorts. However, hefty taxes boost the price of even the cheapest plonk, and a bottle of wine easily doubles the cost of a budget meal.

Turkish wines, mostly made in Cappadocia or along the Aegean coast, are ubiquitous, and many restaurants serve nothing but domestic varieties; the two largest vintners, Doluca and Kavaklıdere, dominate the market, but it's worth asking for local microwinery products, in particular Talay and Corvus from Bozcaada, and Likya label from near Elmalı. The most popular domestic beers, bottled or draught, are Efes Pilsen, Carlsberg and Tuborg, all at about 5 percent; Efes also makes 'Dark' (6.1 percent alcohol) and 'Xtra' (7.5 percent).

The spirit of local choice is *rakı*, similar to Greek ouzo and enjoyed before, during and after a meal, mixed with water and ice.

On the non-alcoholic side, try the freshly-squeezed juices: orange (*portakal*) is the most common but mulberry (*dut*) and pomegranate (*nar*) are even better. Refreshing fresh-

Tea for two

The delightful ritual of Turkish tea drinking launches lasting friendships. It is offered generously and ubiquitously and it is impolite to refuse. If it's too strong and too sweet, ask for *Açık çay, şekersiz* (weak tea without sugar).

fruit smoothies and shakes are also available. Bottled mineral water (*memba suyu*) is the usual alternative to tap water – not recommended except for rural springs designated as potable.

Instant coffee is almost always referred to as Nescafé; if you want something more satisfying, request Turkish coffee, usually served *orta şekerli* (medium sweet) or *çok şekerli* (very sweet). In all resorts, at least one café will be doing European-style espressos and cappuccinos. Tea, *çay*, is more common; it is served in distinctive, tulip-shaped glasses, to which you can add water and sugar, but never milk, as desired.

TO HELP YOU ORDER...

Do you speak English?	**İnglizce biliyormusunz?**
Waiter!	**Lütfen bakarmısınız!**
What do you recommend?	**Ne tavsiye edersiniz?**

...AND READ THE MENU

Meze (Starters)

antep eesi	hot chili purée
barbunya	marinated red kidney beans
cacık	yogurt, cucumber and herb dip
çoban salatası	fine-chopped salad of tomato, cucumber, peppers, onions, olives and parsley
haydarı	thick garlic dip
imam bayıldı	cold baked aubergines with tomato and onion
mücver	courgette frittata
semizotu	purslane leaves, usually mixed with yogurt
sigara böreği	cheese-filled pastry 'cigarettes'
yaprak dolması	stuffed vine leaves

Et (Meat)

döner kebab	sliced roasted lamb
iskender kebab	*döner* drenched in yogurt
karışık ızgara	mixed grill
piliç	roast chicken
pirzola	lamb chops
şiş köfte	grilled lamb meatballs

Balık (Fish), Deniz Ürünleri (Seafood)

ahtapod	octopus	**palamut**	bonito
alabalık	trout	**karides**	prawns
barbunya	red mullet	**kiliç**	swordfish
hamsi	anchovies	**midye**	mussels
kalamar	squid	**sardalya**	sardines

Sebze (Vegetables)

bakla	broad beans	**kuru fasulye**	white haricots
bamya	okra	**nohut**	chickpeas
domates	tomatoes	**patates**	potatoes
ıspanak	spinach	**patlıcan**	aubergine

Tatlı (Dessert)

aşure	Pulse, wheat, fruit and nut pudding
dondurma	Central Asian ice cream
kadayıf	'shredded wheat' in syrup
keşkül	vanilla almond custard
sütlac	rice pudding

Beverages

ayran	yogurt drink	**maden suyu**	mineral water
bira	beer	**viski**	whisky
çay	tea	**suyu**	juice
kahve	coffee	**arap**	wine

PLACES TO EAT

As a guide, we have used the following symbols to give an indication of the price of a full meal for one, excluding alcohol:

$$$$ over £30 ($50) $$ £10–20 ($16–32)
$$$ £20–30 ($32–50) $ below £10 ($16)

AEGEAN COAST

AYVALIK

Deniz Kestanesi $$$ *Karantina Sok. 5–9, tel: 0266-312 3262, www.denizkestanesi.com.* The most elegant (and expensive) seafood restaurant in town. And yes sea urchin (*deniz kestanesi*) – esteemed like Viagra by Turks – features on the menu, along with local specialities like fried *papalina* (a kind of sprat).

BERGAMA

Ticaret Odası Sosyal Tesisleri $$ *In the restored Greek school, 150m uphill from the Ulu Cami, tel: 0232-632 9641.* The only licensed outfit in central Bergama, with municipally subsidized prices for grills and *mezes*. Pleasant indoor environment with big windows overlooking the valley. Cash only.

BOZCAADA (TENEDOS)

Şehir Restaurant $$ *Fishing harbour, tel: 0286-697 8017.* One of the few waterside restaurants with consistently good cooking for meat or fish, and straightforward billing policies. Open most of the year. Cash only.

ÇANAKKALE

Yalova $$$ *Eski Balıkhane Sok 31, off Yalı Caddesi, tel: 0286-217 1045.* Unusual *mezes* and the town's widest range of seafood – though fish prices are also Çanakkale's highest, and you must establish exactly what's included in advance. Dardanelles-view tables upstairs, or in the ground-level conservatory of this historic building. Open all year.

ÇEŞME

İmren $$ *İnkilap Cad. 6/A, tel: 0232-712 7620.* Çeşme's oldest surviving restaurant, founded in 1953 by immigrants from Yugoslavia, has atrium seating and a traditional menu with Balkan touches. The signature dish is *papaz yahnisi* (whole baked carp stuffed with rice). Open all year, daily noon–9pm; cash only.

ESKİ FOÇA

Fokai $$$ *121 Sokak No. 8, behind the castle, tel: 0232-812 2186.* The place for quality fish here, with farmed and fresh items clearly separated, good garnishes or *mezes*, and mostly Turkish clientele. Open all year. Credit cards taken.

GALLIPOLI PENINSULA

Liman $$ *İstiklal Caddesi 67 (south end of waterfront), Eceabat, tel: 0286-814 2755.* Fish and *meze* specialist that's also the only licensed restaurant here – a great sea-view lunch stop during a peninsula tour.

GÖKÇEADA (İMROZ)

BarbaYorgo $–$$ *Tepeköy (Agrídia) village centre, tel: 0286-887 4247.* Island-born Yorgo returned from İstanbul upon retirement to open this enduringly popular Greek-island-style taverna with keenly priced mains and *meze*, accompanied by his own wine (and during the summer season, often live music and dancing).

İZMIR

Asansör Ceneviz Meyhanesi $$$ *Dario Moreno Sokağı, Karataş district, tel: 0232-255 5420.* Take the historic lift up from shoreline level and near the exit is this hugely popular restaurant, with fantastic views across the city to go with delicious seafood and the house kebab.

Deniz $$$ *Atatürk Cad. 188/B (inside İzmir Palas Hotel), tel: 0232-464 4499, www.denizrestaurant.com.tr.* Highly regarded by locals, who return here regularly for speciality seafood dishes like whole fish baked in salt, served in tastefully minimalist surroundings. Good-value set menus; booking advisable. Open all year.

SELÇUK

Ejder $ *Cengiz Topel Caddesi 9, tel: 0232-892 3296.* A prime location in the pedestrian zone opposite a stork-nested aqueduct, plus a well-balanced menu of meat with an east-Anatolian flair, vegetarian platters and fresh *mezes*, combine to make this place a winner. Cash only.

Ocakbaşı $ *Şirince, 5km from Selçuk, tel: 0232-898 3094.* Very friendly, simple, family-run place with stews, *gözleme*, unexpected *meze* like *deniz börülce* and a taste of the (local) wine allowed before committing to a whole bottle. Great views over this historic village from the terrace. Cash only.

YAYLAKÖY

Yılmaz'ınYeri $$ *Top of the pass, Yaylaköy, 9km (5 miles) south of Kuşadası on the road to Söke and Priene, tel: 0256-668 1023.* The best of a cluster of meaty restaurants here, always crowded with locals enjoying traditional *meze* in decent portions, an infinity of kebabs, and a very reasonable wine list.

TURQUOISE COAST

BODRUM

Berk Balık $$ *Cumhuriyet Caddesi 167, Kumbahçe tel: 0252-313 0239.* It can get noise from nearby bars, but this two-storey restaurant offers a roof terrace, sea views and excellent seafood. Open daily noon–midnight.

La Jolla Bistro $$$ *Neyzin Tevfik Cad. 174, opposite Karada Marina, tel: 0252-313 7660*. Small, chic bistro whose menu juggles Mediterranean starters, steakhouse standards and sushi, plus Bodrum's largest selection of wines and coffees. Open all year.

Sünger Pizza $ *Neyzen Tevfik Caddesi 216, Bodrum, tel: 0252-316 0854*. The oldest restaurant in Bodrum, this very busy hangout does salads, pasta and meze as well as excellent pizzas. Open all day every day.

DALYAN

Çağrı Pide Salonu $ *Gülpınar Çarsi Içi, tel: 0252-284 3427*. Despite the name a very decent, licensed all-rounder, with grills and a few well-executed *mezes*, tucked away near the entrance to the local minibus terminal. Cash only.

DATÇA

Fevzi'nin Yeri $$ *Behind centre of Kumluk Beach, tel: 0252-712 9746, www.fevzis.com*. Excellent *meyhane* with a plethora of old-fashioned *meze* platters rarely seen now, cheerful nautical decor and strictly seafood mains. A cult hangout for both locals and visiting Turks. Cash only.

KÖYCEĞIZ

Alila $$ *Lakefront near town centre, tel: 0252-262 1150*. The kitchen staff of this hotel produce unheard-of *mezes* like stewed artichokes, yogurt with coriander greens, and caper shoots marinated in sour pomegranate syrup, while main portions are generous. Very popular so book ahead.

MARMARIS

Ney $$ *26 Sokağı 24, tel: 0252-412 0217*. Installed in an old Greek house with marina views, Ney specialises in home-style platters like *mantı* (Turkish ravioli). Very much a one-person, owner-chef affair with just a few tables, so booking in season advisable.

MEDITERRANEAN COAST

ALANYA

Mahperi Restaurant $$ *Rıhtım Caddesi, tel: 0242-512 5491.* Long-standing harbour-front favourite (since 1947) serving an eclectic mix of everything from omelettes to fish casseroles and fillet steak, with a good selection of vegetarian food as well.

Red Tower Brewery *İskele Caddesi 80, Alanya, tel: 0242-513 6664.* A harbour-front six-storey palace of consumption near the Red Tower – with a microbrewery, lounge bar, plus separate Turkish, seafood and international restaurants.

ANTALYA

Hasanağa $$ *Mescit Sok 15, Kaleiçi, tel: 0242-242 8105.* Popular, durable old-town restaurant, with a characterful indoor dining area, plus a delightful walled courtyard studded with citrus trees. A serve-yourself buffet *meze* table precedes fish or meat mains. Live Turkish music most evenings. Open all year.

Parlak $ *Kazim Özalp Caddesi, Zincirlihan, tel: 0242-241 6553.* Roast-chicken specialists, serving in a large patio, with plenty of *mezes* and dessert as well. Mostly local-patronised. Cash only; open all year.

Vanilla $$$ *Hesapçı Sok. 33, tel: 0242-247 6013, www.vanilla antalya.com.* Chic, cozy Turkish-English-run bistro purveying mainly continental fare (steaks, fish, carpaccio, risotto), with Italian/Asian dishes thrown in. Stylish attached bar. Booking advised in season.

ÇIRALI

Cemil Pansiyon $$ *Shopping 'strip', hamlet centre, tel: 0242-825 7063.* Home-style cooking with good vegetable-based *mezes*, and far better value than the tempting row of upscale beachside restaurants. Credit cards taken for groups, by prior arrangement.

FETHIYE

Meğri Lokantası $$ *Çarşı Caddesi 30, tel: 0252-614 4040*. Decent home-style casseroles and puddings, supposedly open 24hr. Cash only. There is a more blatantly touristy annexe further into the old bazaar at Likya Sokak 8–9 ($$$).

KALKAN

Çiftlik $ *İslamlar village centre, 8km from Kalkan, tel: 0242-838 6055*. Least expensive of a half-dozen trout farm restaurants here; eat your trout withvegetable garnish and flat *yufka* bread while perched above the fish ponds – and a great view. Cash only.

Gironda $$$ *Hasan Altan Caddesi 28, Yalıboyu, tel: 0242-844 1298*. A beautiful courtyard bar and rooftop terrace with great Ottoman and international food, a good winecellar, all wrapped up in an old Greek building festooned in bougainvillaea.

Korsan Meze $$$ *Harbour front, tel: 0242-844 3622*. As implied by the name, very creative mezes precede mains, but as with all Kalkan restaurants, clarify any hidden charges in advance. Open May–Oct. Credit cards accepted.

Kuru'nin Yeri $ *3.5km (2 miles) east of Kalkan, en route Kaputaş beach, tel: 0242-844 3848*. Best of a trio of roadside restaurants clustered here, doling out inexpensive homestyle dishes like *mantı* (ravioli), *nohutlu et* (chickpeas with meat chunks), *şakşuka* and corn bread. Open all year. Cash only.

KAYA KÖYU

Cin Bal $ *Signposted at easterly approach to village, tel: 0252-618 0066*. This is a *kendin pişin kendin ye* place, where you buy superb lamb by the kilo and then cook it yourself at a tableside brazier. Open all year. Cash only.

Sarnıç $$$ *Edge of ruined village, tel: 0252-618 0153*. Most successful of several upscale restaurants in the area, with quality live music some evenings and table service on a fieldstoned courtyard. The kitchen occupies one of the few restored houses here, downstairs from an informal museum of local ethnographic finds. Open most of year. Credit cards accepted.

KAŞ

Bahçe $$ *Top of Uzun Çarşı, behind Lion Tomb, tel: 0242-836 2370.* The best cold or hot *meze* in town, served in the garden (*bahçe*); mains are less exciting. The seafood annexe just opposite (tel: 0242-836-2779; $$$) is also excellent, with unusual *mezes* like marinated sea-bass fillet. Both open May to early November.

Sultan Garden $$–$$$ *Hükümet Caddesi, opposite coast guard station, tel: 0242-836 3762.* The place for a special night out, featuring less common *meze* platters like *paçanga böreği* (turnovers with *pastırma*, tomato, cheese), plus lamb-based mains. Outdoor terrace open May–Oct.

ÖLÜDENIZ

Kumsal Pide $ *Belceğiz esplanade, southeast end, tel: 0252-617 0058.* Fabulous *pide* in large portions and equally big *meze* platters at startlingly normal prices. Substantial local clientele, so open most of the year. Licensed. Cash only.

PATARA

Tlos Restaurant (Bolu'lu Osman Usta) $ *Centre of Gelemiş resort area, tel: 0242-843 5135.* Big portions of traditional home-style casserole food and fry-ups like liver and onions, done by a chef from Bolu. Very good value. Cash only; unlicensed.

SIDE

Orfoz $$ *Liman Caddesi 58, tel: 0242-753 1362.* Shady harbour-front restaurant with wonderful views of the sunset and excellent seafood and steaks – no wonder that this favourite has survived while others around it have come and gone.

A–Z TRAVEL TIPS

A Summary of Practical Information

A

ACCOMMODATION

The Turkish coast has abundant accommodation, largely falling into two categories: hotels *(oteller)*, extending to massive self-contained complexes, or guest houses *(pansiyonlar)* which can mean simple, rock-bottom accommodation or characterful, comfortable bed-and-breakfast-type lodgings. In Bozcaada, Ayvalık, Eski Foça, Alaçatı and Antalya, many delightfully restored Ottoman mansions operate as small boutique hotels, but elsewhere beware – the Turkish designation *butik* is much (ab)used to justify charging over the odds at any establishment with a bit of stone cladding outside, and cast-iron bed-frames inside. There are also villas and apartments with pools available; other villas enjoy quiet, rural, locations, but may not have pools. Exclusive Escapes (tel: +44 (0)20-8605 3500, www.exclusiveescapes.co.uk) is a UK-based package operator working with some of the finest hotels and villas along the coast between Datça and Kaş. A good directory of boutique hotels can be found at www.boutiqueandsmallhotels.com.

All hotels are officially rated on a scale equivalent to a one-to-five-star system, though some restoration or boutique projects fall in the *özel* (special) category. Technically, rating is based on amenities offered (pool, restaurant, lifts, etc.) but does not reflect charm or ambience. Breakfast – 'traditional' Turkish in simpler places, buffet-style with 'western' options in multi-starred establishments – is

I have a reservation.	**Reservasyonim var.**
I'd like a single/double room.	**Tek/çift yataklı bir oda istiyorum.**
With shower	**Duşlu**
What is the price per night?	**Bir gecelik oda ücreti ne kadar?**
Can I see the room?	**Bakabılırmıyım?**

usually included in quoted rates. Many establishments have single/twin beds only; if you want a double bed, request a *fransiz yatak* ('French' bed), not always available. Many hotels use solar panels, so if travelling out of season check if they have year-round hot water and central heating. Advance reservations are highly advisable at peak season, and weekends in any month.

Many foreign-owned holiday homes are available for rent: try www.holidaylettings.co.uk, www.ownersdirect.co.uk and www.holiday-rentals.co.uk.

AIRPORTS *(havaalanlari;* see also GETTING THERE)

Air travellers are spoiled for choice, with five airports scattered along the coast. İzmir and Antalya have year-round scheduled services (both full price and low-cost) from a variety of European cities, plus there are no-frills flights to Bodrum and Dalaman on the Aegean and Mediterranean coasts respectively. In summer, charter flights provide additional services to all of the above. The small Gazipaşa airport near Alanya began accepting low-cost flights in 2011.

B

BICYCLE AND SCOOTER HIRE

Bicycle-hire outlets prove scarce, and given often challenging road conditions, cycling isn't especially recommended. A better bet are off-road mountain-biking expeditions provided by adventure outfitters. Scooter outlets are somewhat more common, but again strictly at your own risk. Show your driver's licence, make sure the rates include insurance and insist on being provided with a helmet.

BUDGETING FOR YOUR TRIP

While Turkey is still good value, the country is not ultra-cheap. Accommodation is reasonably priced, although notably more expensive in İzmir, Bodrum and Antalya than elsewhere. Prices start at around US$70/£42 a night for a double room in a good *pansiyon*, ranging up to US$400/£250 a night for a luxury 5-star hotel. Car hire prices vary sharply (see below); petrol is expensive at over $2/£1.30 per litre, yet local transport remains affordable; online specials for domestic air tickets can often nearly match bus fares.

You can eat inexpensively by patronising unlicensed backstreet kebab shops and roadside *gözleme* stalls, but otherwise meals tend to cost what they do in most of the European Mediterranean. Generally, two people can dine extremely well for about $60/£36 and have a pleasant, simple meal for about $35/£22 (with beer, not wine) and a light snack for under $20/£13. Seafood is considerably more expensive than meat, reaching pan-Mediterranean prices in major resorts. Beer is on the cheap side, but wine and *rakı* are dear. Coffee is much more expensive than tea, especially if it's cappuccino or espresso.

C

CAMPING *(kamping)*

Camping is possible at a handful of designated sites along the Aegean and Mediterranean coasts, and 'free lance' along the Lycian Way and St Paul Trail. The most pleasant formal sites, especially if you have a caravan or camper-van, are those run by the Ministry of Forestry – look for yellow lettering on brown wooden signs.

CAR HIRE *(OTO kİraLama)*

To hire a car, you must be over 21 and have had a licence for a year. You will also need a credit card for the damages deposit. The major companies all have outlets in Turkey and there are also many local hire-car agencies. Antalya, Bodrum, Dalaman airport and (sometimes) İzmir airport are the least expensive places to pick up a car; İstanbul, Marmaris, Kuşadası, Çeşme and anywhere in the east are the most expensive. Booking online will often be much cheaper, especially for longer periods. Order child seats upon booking, and at pick-up check that you have a full set of spares (punctures are common). If you have an accident when driving in Turkey, notify the police immediately; insurance claims are invalid unless accompanied by an official accident report (*kaza raporu*).

The following UK/US-based websites may be useful:

www.comparecarrentals.co.uk

www.auto-europe.co.uk/.com

www.carhire3000.com

www.skycars.co.uk

www.affordablecarehire.co.uk

CLIMATE

There are several hundred kilometres difference in latitude between Çanakkale and the Mediterranean, and thousands of metres of difference in altitude between the coast and the mountains that soar vertically above them, all of which affects climate. Generally, though, the coast is cool and damp in winter, almost perfect in spring and autumn and bakingly hot in summer. The higher mountains get plenty of snow, with critical passes iced up.

İzmir:	J	F	M	A	M	J	J	A	S	O	N	D
°C max	13	14	17	21	26	31	33	33	29	24	19	14
°C min	4	4	6	9	13	17	21	21	17	13	9	6
°F max	55	57	63	70	79	87	92	92	85	76	67	58
°F min	39	40	43	49	56	63	69	69	62	55	49	42

Antalya:	J	F	M	A	M	J	J	A	S	O	N	D
°C max	15	16	18	21	26	30	34	33	31	27	22	17
°C min	6	7	8	11	16	19	23	22	19	15	11	8
°F max	59	61	65	70	79	86	94	92	88	81	72	63
°F min	43	45	47	52	61	67	74	72	67	59	52	47

CLOTHING

Although you do see plenty of Turkish women in the resorts wearing skimpy tops and short skirts, it is good manners to leave beachwear – and bare male torsos – on the beach and cover up when you go into town. Shorts are fine, but not too short; miniskirts should be respectable and t-shirts should ideally cover both shoulders and navels. General summer in-town apparel is lightweight trousers and short-sleeved button-down or polo shirts for men, trousers and blouses, skirts, or dresses for women. When visiting archaeological sites or hiking the backcountry, you need heavier-duty walking shoes or boots. A hat and sunglasses are essentials in summer. In the evening men rarely need formal wear – smart casual is enough for most restaurants.

In winter, bring light pullovers and something waterproof; inland and transiting İstanbul, you may need full-on winter gear.

CRIME AND SAFETY

The crime rate in Turkey is relatively low but you do need to watch out for pickpockets or purse-snatchers in crowded markets and bars, or in the metro/tram if transiting İstanbul. Most people are honest but some tradesmen consider foreigners fair game, e.g. quoting a price initially in Turkish lira and then, wrapping the goods, claiming it was in euro. Or there's the occasional taxi driver who takes you for an unnecessary drive halfway round Turkey or uses sleight of hand to short-change you, or accuse you of not paying in full. Try to find out what an appropriate price is beforehand, and make sure you always have plenty of small change.

There are extremely harsh penalties for drug possession in Turkey, and the export of antiquities without a proper permit is illegal. And remember that while most Turks tolerate alcohol, and many do drink, devout Muslims do not. The sight of drunken tourists being sick in the gutters, throwing punches at fellow tourists and being carted off to hospital to have their stomachs pumped (all common occurrences in some resorts) is not one to endear them to their hosts.

D

DRIVING

Turkey's roads are not for the faint of heart and you need to drive defensively at all times. While some major highways, including the country's growing number of toll motorways, are well designed and well maintained, many roads are poorly paved, poorly marked and lit, erratically signposted and dangerously curvy and narrow, with few crash barriers on cliff roads. Turks drive fast and often recklessly – expect sudden stops, heedless pulling out of side roads, turns without signals, overtaking on all sides. In rural areas, you are likely to come upon flocks of sheep and goats in the road, as well as elderly and overloaded trucks, children playing football or donkey carts headed down the carriageway in the wrong direction. All of these pose an extra hazard at night, especially with the frequent presence of unlit vehicles. Traffic lights go straight from red to green; a flashing yellow arrow means you can turn right if the road is clear even if the main light is red.

You may drive on your national driver's licence for up to three months, but an IDP is most useful for flashing at the many control points. If bringing a car into Turkey, you will need the logbook, proof of ownership, a Green Card and carnet. Check you are comprehensively insured. An official nationality sticker must be displayed at the rear of the vehicle, and the vehicle equipped with flares, a red breakdown-warning triangle, and a full set of spares (including bulbs).

Drive on the right, pass on the left and give way to the right, even on roundabouts. Speed limits are 120km/h (70mph) on motorways, 90km/h (55mph), or 80km (50mph) for big vans or caravans on rural roads; 50km/h (30mph) or 40km/h (25mp/h) if towing something in town. Drivers and all passengers must wear seat belts, and motorcyclists must wear helmets. Blood-alcohol limits are in line with European countries – 50mg alcohol per 100ml of blood – so just two beers will put you over the limit. Traffic control points and radar speed traps are common, particularly at the entrance to towns;

Park Yapılmaz/Edilmez	No Parking
Durmak Yasaktır	No Stopping
Yol Yapımı	Men Working (Road Works)
Dikkat	Danger
Yavaş	Slow Down
Tek Yön	One-way
Giremez	No Entry
Şehir Merkezi	Town Centre

Some useful phrases:

Driving licence	**Şoförlük ruhsatiyesi**
Petrol	**Benzin**
Petrol station	**Benzin ıstasyonu**
Oil	**Motor yağı**
Tyre	**Lâstik**
Brakes	**Frenler**
It does not work.	**Calismiyor.**
Fill the tank, please.	**Doldurum, lütfen.**
I've had a breakdown.	**Arabam arızalandı.**
There's been an accident.	**Bir kaza oldu.**

foreigners, especially in rental vehicles, are likely to be waved through.

Petrol *(benzin)* and diesel *(mazot)* are readily available around larger towns and resorts, sometimes on a 24-hr basis; however, stations can be far apart in eastern Turkey. Petrol is available three grades: super, normal and lead-free fuel *(kurşunsuz)*, the latter rarer in rural districts; so-called euro-diesel is more efficient than standard. In most of the country, you can pay for fuel by credit card.

E

ELECTRICITY

220V/50Hz; continental-style two round-pin plugs.

EMBASSIES AND CONSULATES

Consulates (in İstanbul unless otherwise stated)
Australia: 2nd Floor, Suzer Plaza, Asker Ocağı Cad.15, Elmadağ, tel: 0212-243 1333; **Canada:** İstiklâl Caddesi 373/5, Beyoğlu, tel: 0212-251 9838; **Ireland:** Ali Riza Gürcan Caddesi, Meridyen İş Merkezi Kat 4, no, 417, tel: 0212-482 1862; **UK:** Mesrutiyet Cad. 34, Tepebaşı, Beyoğlu, tel: 0212-293 7540; in Antalya: Gürsu Mah. 324 Sok. 6, Konyaaltı, tel: 0242-228 2811; in Bodrum: Cafer Paşa Caddesi, İkinci Emsan Evleri 7, tel: 0252-313 0021; in Fethiye, Atatürk Caddesi, Likya İş Merkezi, Kat 2, 202, tel: 0252- 614 6302; in İzmir: 1442 Sok. 49, Alsancak, tel: 0232-463 5151; and in Marmaris: Barbaros Caddesi 11, tel: 0252-412 6486; **US:** Kaplıcalar Mevkii 2, İstinye, tel: 0212-335 9000.

Embassies in Ankara

Australia: Nenehatun Cad. 83, Gaziosmanpaşa, tel: 0312-459 9500; **Canada:** Cinnah Cad. 58, Çankaya, tel: 0312-409 2712; **New Zealand:** Iran Cad. 13/4, Kavaklıdere, tel: 0312-467 9054; **UK:** Şehit Ersan Cad. 46/A, Cankaya, tel: 0312-455 3344; **US:** Atatürk Bulv. 110, Kavaklıdere, tel: 0312-455 5555.

EMERGENCY NUMBERS

154 Traffic police
155 Police, general (you will be directed to a specialised extension if necessary)
110 Urban fire department
112 Ambulance

Help!	**Imdat!**
I am ill.	**Hastayım.**
Call a doctor.	**Doktor cagirim.**
Where is the hospital?	**Nerede hastane?**

G

GAY AND LESBIAN TRAVELLERS

Although homosexual activity between consenting adults over age 18 is legal, Turks are generally intolerant of gay lifestyles; it is illegal to print and distribute material promoting homosexuality. Members of the same sex travel and socialise together, Turkish men often greet each other with a (cheek) kiss and make physical contact with one another, so gay couples should feel quite comfortable travelling together. However, sexually charged contact could result in violence, and attacks on gay or transgender individuals have increased in recent years. Bodrum, Alanya, Antalya and Marmaris are considered the most gay-friendly resorts.

GETTING THERE (see also AIRPORTS)

By air. A few major international carriers (including BA and Aer Lingus) fly direct to İzmir. In summer, there are many additional direct flights (no-frills scheduled and charter) to Dalaman, Bodrum and Antalya. The national carrier, Turkish Airlines (THY, www.thy.com), provides direct services across the globe. From the UK, Thomas Cook and Thomson offer flight-only charter deals in season, and low-cost carriers such as easyJet (www.easyjet.com), Pegasus Air (www.flypgs.com), Anadolujet (www.anadolujet.com) and Jet2 (www.jet2.com) provide flights throughout the year.

By land. Travelling from other European cities to İstanbul by train is long (about 72 hours from London) and far more expensive than a flight, only really worth it if you plan to stop en route. Through tickets from the UK are no longer even sold; the best single website for planning is www.seat61.com. There are no trains along the coast, limited services from İstanbul to İzmir, and from there southeast to Selçuk and Denizli (for Pamukkale).

It takes up to four days to drive to Turkey from most of Western Europe. The most direct all-land route from the UK goes via Belgium, Germany, Austria, Hungary and Bulgaria. Alternatively, drive to Italy and then to Greece or Turkey by ferry.

By sea. Ferries run from both Ancona and Brindisi in Italy to Çeşme, near İzmir – the last surviving long-haul sea-links. Marmara Lines connects Ancona with Çeşme from late May to mid-September only, while Mesline MedEuropean Seaways links Brindisi with Çeşme at roughly the same period; full information is available on www.cemar.it. There are also (often seasonal) services from the Greek islands opposite to various Turkish resort-ports; www.feribot.net is a useful information and booking resource.

GUIDES AND TOURS

There are thousands of tours and guides on offer, from full-blown package excursions, to day-trips sold by agencies in the resorts, to state-licensed archaeological/cultural guides, or small boys hanging around sights hoping for a tip.

H

HEALTH AND MEDICAL CARE

You don't need any inoculations for Turkey and there are no serious health risks in the regions covered by this guide. The most common visitor problems are stomach upsets or sunburn and/or heat stroke. All are easily avoided – keep hands washed and eat only freshly cooked, hygienically stored food; wear a hat and sunblock and drink plenty of water. Tap water is heavily chlorinated and not exactly tasty; restaurants always offer inexpensive bottled water. Rural springs are labelled *içilir*, *içibelir* or *içme suyu* (all meaning 'drinkable') or *içilmez* ('not drinkable'). Use insect repellent in the evenings; hotels and *pansiyons* usually supply mosquito nets or electric repellent pads when necessary.

Turkish pharmacies are well supplied, and pharmacists usually well trained and happy to provide advice. Pharmacies are open dur-

ing normal business hours; in each town, one pharmacy stays open
late and on Sundays – the rota is posted in all pharmacies.

Your hotel will be able to get you a doctor if necessary. The quality of medical care is generally good. Make sure you have travel insurance that will cover any medical treatment you may need; the
European Health Insurance Card (EHIC) is not valid in Turkey. You
may be asked to pay for treatment upfront, so keep receipts for re-
imbursement.

Where can I find a doctor/ dentist?	**Nereden bir doktor/ bir disci bulabilirim?**
Where is the nearest pharmacy?	**En yakin eczane nerededir?**
Sunburn	**Güneş yanğı**
Fever	**Ateş**
Stomach ache	**Karnağrısı**

L

LANGUAGE

English is widely spoken in resorts but even a few words of Turkish
are greatly appreciated. The language uses a modified Roman alpha-
bet and pronunciation is very predictable as long as you know what
to do with the accents, and letters that vary from English values:

c like j in jam

ç like ch in chip

ğ almost silent, lengthening the preceding vowel

h always pronounced

ı like **the sound between b and l in 'probable'**

j like s in pleasure

ö like ur in fur

ş like sh in shell

ü like ew in few

Some basic words and phrases:

Good morning	**Günaydın**	Goon-eye-DUHN
Please	**Lütfen**	LEWT-fen
Thank you	**Teşekkür ederim**	TEH-sheh-kur eh-dey-REEM
Bon appetit	**Afiyet olsun**	
Cheers!	**Şerefe!**	
You're welcome	**Bir şey değil**	
Excuse me	**Özür dilerim**	Oh-ZEWR deel-air-eem
Where is...?	**Nerede...?**	Neh-re-de...?
I don't understand	**Anlamıyorum**	Ahn-LAH-muh-yohr-um
I'd like...	**İstiyorum...**	EES-tee-yohr-ruhm
How much is that?	**Bu ne kadar?**	boo neh kaddar?
Tuvalet var mı?	**Is there a toilet here?**	
OK	**Tamam**	
Yes/No	**Evet/Hayır**	

Numbers:

one	**bir**	beer
two	**iki**	ee-KEE
three	**üç**	ooch
four	**dört**	duhrt
five	**beş**	besh
six	**altı**	ahl-TUH
seven	**yedi**	YED-dee
eight	**sekiz**	sek-KEEZ
nine	**dokuz**	doh-KOOZ
ten	**on**	ohn
hundred	**yüz**	yewz

Days of the week:

Monday	**Pazartesi**	Pah-ZAHR-teh-see
Tuesday	**Salı**	SAL-luh
Wednesday	**Çarşamba**	Char-shahm-BAH
Thursday	**Perşembe**	Pae-shem-BEH
Friday	**Cuma**	Joo-MAH
Saturday	**Cumartesi**	Joo-MAHR-teh-see
Sunday	**Pazar**	Pah-ZAHR

MAPS

Good regional maps are hard to find. Consider buying one before you leave home; the best currently available is Reise Know-How's 1:700,000-scale *Western Turkey Mediterranean Coast and Cyprus*, which covers the entire southern and western third of the country. Locally, Sabri Aydal's reliable 1:250,000 products for Lycia and Pamphylia are available at better bookshops and museums.

MEDIA

Some foreign-language newspapers are sold at a sharp markup from newsstands in larger resorts. The two local English-language dailies are the *Hürriyet Daily News* (www.hurriyetdailynews.com) and the superior *Today's Zaman* (www.todayszaman.com). News in English is broadcast on CNN, BBC World and Al Jazeera; better hotels offer a satellite package including these, as well as the private Digitürk network's English-language CNBC-e and E2 channels.

MONEY

The unit of currency is the Türk Lirası (TL, Turkish Lira); 1TL is broken into 100 kuruş, which exist in coins of 1, 5, 10, 25 and 50 kuruş, plus 1 TL. Notes come in denominations of 5, 10, 20, 50, 100 and 200TL.

Most travellers obtain cash either through the ubiquitous ATMs, or exchange sterling, euro or US$ bills at dedicated foreign-exchange booths (*döviz burolar*); these are open much longer hours than banks, and charge no commision, though usually offer a poorer rate. Credit/debit cards are useful for air ticket and petrol purchase; most brands are accepted. Payment in foreign currency is happily accepted for purchase of valuable souvenirs (eg carpets).

OPENING TIMES

In general, hours are: archaeological sites, 8.30am–6.30pm daily in summer (with many variations); government offices, 8.30am–12.30pm and 1.30–5.30pm, Mon–Fri (tourist offices are often open on week-ends too); museums, 8.30/9am–5.30/6pm Tue–Sun (with many vari-ations); restaurants, noon–2.30 or 3pm for lunch, 7 or 7.30pm–10.30 or 11pm for dinner; shops, 9am–7pm (much later in some resorts).

POLICE *(polis)*

Turkey has several different types of police. Municipal *polis* deal with petty crime, traffic, parking and other day-to-day matters; the national *Jandarma*, actually a branch of the army, handle serious crime and civil unrest and protect government figures; *Trafik Polis* monitor highways plus town streets; the *Belediye Zabıtası* (market police) patrol market areas with an eye out for crooks; and the *Tur-izm Polis*, who should speak English, are found in busy tourist areas.

Where's the nearest police station?   **En yakın karakol nerede?**

POST OFFICES

Look for the PTT sign to find a post office. In the major cities and resorts, the central post office is open 8am–midnight; others are open 8.30am–12.30pm and 1.30–5.30pm. Express service is faster but much more expensive than the reliable but slow standard post; use courier companies for anything precious. Post offices also offer metered counter-telephone service.

PUBLIC HOLIDAYS

Turkey observes the following offical holidays:

New Year's Day	**1 January**
National Independence and Children's Day	**23 April**
Atatürk's Birthday, Youth and Sports Day	**19 May**
Victory Day	**30 August**
Republic Day (anniversary of the declaration of the Turkish Republic)	**29 October**
Anniversary of Atatürk's death	**10 November**

The most important Islamic holidays, which drift backward 11 days annually relative to the western calendar, are Şeker Bayramı (end of Ramazan), falling in mid-summer until 2015, and Kurban Bayramı (Festival of the Sacrifice), occurring lately in mid-autumn. Both are multi-day festivals, and the country effectively shuts down for the duration as everyone who can goes on holiday. Many restaurants close during Ramazan at midday, except in tourist resorts.

R

RELIGION

Turkey is 99 percent Muslim. Religious sentiment has been on the rise in recent years – 62 percent of Turkish women now wear some sort of head covering. Non-Muslims are welcome to visit mosques, though often not during prayers. Visitors must remove their shoes (at larger mosques, an attendant will check them; elsewhere, there's a rack inside the door on which to place them). Men and women should cover their legs and upper arms (no shorts, exposed knees or sleeveless tops) and women should cover their heads.

T

TELEPHONES

Turkey's mobile phone networks offer widespread coverage; they use the European operating system, so North Americans will need a tri-band phone. Foreign visitors should not roam on their home SIM for anything other than texting; since Turkish networks are not subject to EU roaming caps, making or receiving voice calls is extortionately expensive. Instead, purchase a local pay-as-you-go SIM card (they start from around 20TL) or, for somewhat dearer rates, an international roaming SIM card (www.gosim.co.uk).

Because of the prevalence of mobile use, there are fewer public phones now. They are usually blue, and take phone cards (from post offices and newsstands) or credit cards. Instructions are available in several languages. For more quiet, go to a TT (Türk Telekom) premises. Local calls are quite cheap. To call internationally, dial 00, then the country code. Calling Turkey from abroad, its country code is 90; omit the initial zero of the 11-digit Turkish land or mobile number. Avoid phoning from your hotel room, as surcharges are horrendous.

TIME ZONES

Turkey is 2 hours ahead of Greenwich Mean Time (GMT). It observes Daylight Savings Time as in Europe: 1 hour forward the last Sunday in March, reverting to standard time the last Sunday in October.

New York	London	**Turkey**	Sydney	Los Angeles
5am	10am	**noon**	9pm	2am

TIPPING

Tip bellhops about 2TL a bag, and leave about 1TL per day of stay for a hotel chambermaid. In many small hotels and *pansiyons*, front-desk staff double up as cleaners and breakfast waiters, so leave a generous tip upon departure. In taxis, simply round up the total. Tour guides and excursion-boat operators usually expect 15–25TL per day of friendly service. In non-fancy restaurants where no service charge or *garsoniye* ('waiter charge') is levied, 10 percent of the bill is fine; in fancier places, mandatory service charges can exceed 20 percent of the bill, but leave a bit extra if service has been good.

TOILETS *(tuvaletler)*

Public toilets are increasingly kept clean and tidy by a full-time warden, who will charge users between 50 kuruş and 1TL. The most savoury loos are at archaeological sites and museums, cafés or restaurants, and petrol stations. Most offer a mix of Western-style and oriental squat toilets. All have little squirter-pipes aimed your nether parts, as local custom requires cleansing with running water. Carry a bit of toilet paper with you to blot yourself dry, and (usually) deposit this in a basket next to the basin, not in it. The gents' toilet is designated *bay(lar)*, the ladies' *bayan(lar)*.

TOURIST INFORMATION

The official Turkish Tourism websites are www.goturkey.com, www.tourismturkey.org and www.gototurkey.co.uk.

Turkish Tourist Offices abroad
UK: 4th Floor, 29–30 St James' Street, London SW1A 1HB, tel: 020-7839 7778. **US:** 821 United Nations Plaza, New York, NY 10017, tel: 212-687-2194

Tourist offices in Turkey
There are minimally helpful offices in Alanya, Antalya, Ayvalık, Bodrum, Çanakkale, Çeşme, Dalaman Airport, Fethiye, İzmir, Kaş, Kuşadası, Marmaris and Selçuk.

TRANSPORT

It is perfectly possible to holiday along the Turkish coast without your own transport, using a combination of excursions, taxis, long-distance buses, and minibuses that cover set routes between the local villages.

Long-distance buses furnish the main links between cities and towns along the coast. Towns of any size has at least one *otogar* (bus station). As each bus company posts its own timetable, finding out who goes where when can be a laborious process.

Dolmuşes (shared taxi-vans) operate in the larger resorts, and serve as the main transport between smaller villages, and to remote beaches or ruins. They ply established routes, Stops are marked with a 'D' sign. Yellow taxis are everwhere; make sure the meter is running and visible, and that the driver understands where you want to go (write it down to avoid misunderstanding). For trips to remote sites, it is worth doing a flat-rate deal for the morning or day.

When is the next bus to…?	**Bir sonraki otobüs kaçta kalkıyor…?**
A ticket to […]	**Bir bilet [….]'a**
What time does it leave?	**Kaçta kalkiyor?**
How long does it take?	**Ne kadar surebilir?**
How much does it cost?	**Ne kadar?**

VISAS AND ENTRY REQUIREMENTS

Tourist visa requirements and costs vary substantially according to your nationality. All travellers need a passport valid for at least six months. Visas for 90 days are usually granted on entry and in the case of the US and UK the fee is £10/$US20.

Turkish regulations permit visitors to bring all personal effects, including one camera, one music system (eg iPod), one personal computer and one video player. Duty-free import limits for luxury consumables include 5 litres of wine or spirits, 200 cigarettes, 50 cigars, and 200g of tobacco, 1.5kg coffee, 500g of tea and 1kg of chocolate. Exiting Turkey into the EU (particularly Greece), there is a duty-free limit for souvenir purchases. It is an offence to attempt to export 'antiquities', whose exact definition is vague but can include very old carpets. Reputable dealers will prepare a document for you stating that the purchased item is not an antiquity.

WEBSITES AND INTERNET ACCESS

www.turkeytravelplanner.com American-orientated site with loads of practical tips and links to vetted service providers.
www.trekkinginturkey.com Information on major trekking areas.
www.turkeycentral.com Useful portal with good links.
www.mymerhaba.com Authoritative, with good events listings.
www.bodrumlife.com
www.enjoykalkan.com
www.walkizmir.com
Wi-Fi zones are ubiquitous in bars and restaurants, and even surprisingly modest *pansiyons* will have a signal (usually free), in common areas if not every room; luxury hotels may well charge for use.

YOUTH HOSTELS

Pansiyons in Turkey are so widespread that hostels per se are restricted to backpacker meccas such as Kuşadası, Fethiye, Çanakkale and Köyceğiz. Along the Lycian coast, interesting adaptations of these – getting around a ban on 'permanent' buildings in protected areas – are the so-called 'treehouse' lodges, particularly at Olympos, near Ölüdeniz and elsewhere along the Lycian Way.

Recommended Hotels

Given limited space, only those hotels that we can whole-heartedly recommend are listed – they must have great character, provide excellent value, be well located, particularly friendly or unusually well equipped with amenities.

The symbols below indicate the price range for a double room with bath, including breakfast, in high season; costs will be considerably lower at other times, although many coastal hotels close between November and April.

$$$$$	above £200 ($325)
$$$$	£130–200 ($210–325)
$$$	£80–130 ($130–210)
$$	£50–80 ($80–130)
$	below £50 ($80)

AEGEAN COAST

ASSOS (BEHRAMKALE)

Berceste $$$ *Sivrice Feneri, Bektaş Köyü, 10km west of Assos, tel: 0286-723 4616, www.bercestehotel.com.* Stone walls, flagged floors and wooden beams characterise this hillside guesthouse with fabulous views towards Lésvos. There's a pebble beach 400m downhill. Half-board only.

Biber Evi $$$$ *Behramkale square, tel: 0286-721 7410, www.biber evi.com.* Peppers (*biberler*) are the theme here – 20 types in the garden, tiles depicting them in the 6 units. Fittings carved from recycled wood; a fireplace-lounge-bar is the big winter hit, though the upper terrace is the *pièce de resistance*. Half-board obligatory in season.

AYVALİK

Sızma Han $$$ *Gümrük Caddesi, İkinci Sok 49, tel: 0266-312 7700, www.butiksizmahan.com.* Beautifully redone olive mill from

1908; tastefully modern rooms with veneer floors and furniture preserve stone pointing. Common areas include a competent, seafood-strong terrace restaurant and a fireplace lounge. Booking essential.

BOZCAADA (TENEDOS)

Katina $$$ *Yirmi Eylül Caddesi, Kısa Sokağı, near church, tel: 0286-697 0242, www.katinaas.com.* Designer hotel occupying two former Greek houses; rooms vary save for grey-wood lattice ceilings throughout. Breakfast at tables in the lane under the vines, or at the cozy café opposite. Open April–Oct.

ÇANAKKALE

Kervansaray $$$ *Fetvane Sok 13, tel: 0286-217 8192, www.anzac hotel.com/kervansaray.htm.* Justifiably popular hotel comprising a 1903-vintage judge's mansion and a less distinguished rear annexe. Best of the mansion rooms with their mock Belle-Époque furnishings are no. 206 or 207, overlooking the garden.

ÇEŞME PENINSULA

Sheraton Çeşme $$$$ *Sifme Caddesi 35, Ilıca, tel: 0232-723 1240, www.sheratoncesme.com.* This Sheraton, like others in the chain, is an oasis of sumptuous luxury, with a private beach, kids' programs and one of the best spas in the area.

Taş Otel $$$$ *Kemalpaşa Caddesi, Alaçatı, tel: 0232-716 7772, www.tasotel.com.* This former Greek village near Çeşme has a dozen boutique restoration inns; this, installed in an 1890s mansion, was the first and still about the best. Breakfast terrace overlooks the lawn-set pool; just 7 rooms, so bookings are mandatory. Open all year.

ESKİ FOÇA

Lola 38 $$$ *Reha Midilli 140, Küçükdeniz Bay, tel: 0532-617 2035 or 0232-812 3809.* Boutique hotel occupying a former Orthodox priest's mansion, with two upstairs units retaining their original ceilings and fittings. Three more rooms occupy stone outbuildings in the back garden with its lawn-bar, venue for scrumptious breakfasts.

GALLIPOLI PENINSULA

Gallipoli Houses $$$ *Kocadere village, 7km north of Kabatepe road, tel: 0286-814 2650, www.gallipoli.com.tr.* A restored main house and newer garden units offer boutique comfort. Breakfasts are hearty, while suppers are gourmet standard, with a full regional wine cellar. Half board only Mon–Fri.

İZMİR

Beyond $$$–$$$$ *1376 Cad. 5, Alsancak, İzmir, tel: 0232-463 0585, www.hotelbeyond.com.* This trendy place near the seafront makes slightly disconcerting use of six colours in the rooms (supposedly for Chakra therapy), but it's stylish, comfortable and has plentiful amenities for business travellers, including a good restaurant.

Crowne Plaza İzmir $$$ *İnciraltı Caddesi 67, Balçova, İzmir, tel: 0232-292 1300, http://cpizmir.com.* One of the best local luxury hotels, a round reflective tower in a quiet seafront location with all expected facilities (including the Agamemnon Spa) and a regular shuttle into the city centre.

KUŞADASI

Kismet $$$ *Gazi Beğendi Bulvarı 1, Turkmen Mahallesi, Kuşadası, tel: 0256-618 1290, www.kismet.com.tr.* Built in 1966 by Princess Hümeyra Özbaş (1917–2000), a grand-daughter of the last sultan, this venerable hotel set on its own peninsula is still run by her descendants. Airy rooms and suites; large pool. Open all year.

Muses House $$$ *Kırazlı village, House 158, 11km east of Kuşadası, tel: 0256-667 1125, www.museshouse.com.* In one of the loveliest Aegean valleys, a very civilised, five-room boutique inn with plenty of homey communal areas (including scholarly library and garden-pool). Half-board available. Open Apr–Oct.

PAMUKKALE

Venüs $ *Hasan Tahsin Caddesi 16, Pamukkale Köyü, tel: 0258-272 2152, www.venushotel.net*. Friendly family-run hotel plushly furnished with kilims and traditional furniture; small garden, fireplace-lounge and pool. The garden restaurant has a good selection of vegetarian food.

SELÇUK

Kalehan $$ *North end of main through road (Highway 550), Selçuk, tel: 0232-892 6154, www.kalehan.com*. Highest-standard hotel in Selçuk, with antiques and mock-Ottoman decor wedded to modern conveniences, and a competent restaurant. Extensive pool-garden with views up to the castle just behind. Open all year.

Nişanyan Hotel $$$–$$$$ *Şirince village 5km east of Selçuk, top of south slope, tel: 0232-898 3208, www.nisanyan.com*. Superbly atmospheric outfit comprising a five-room central building with sweeping views; three restored village houses suitable for families just below; a five-unit tower; and the idyllic İlyastepe cottages uphill, set amongst terraces of lavender, orchards and ponds. Spring-fed pool; restaurant.

TURQUOISE COAST

BODRUM AND PENINSULA

Aegean Gate $$ *Akçabük Mevki, Kumbahçe Mahallesi, Güvercin Sokağı 2, Bodrum, tel: 0252-316 7853, www.aegeangatehotel.com*. Beautiful Irish-owned mini-hotel (2 apartments and 4 suites, each fitting 3) in a dramatically rocky setting about 10 minutes from Bodrum centre; top marks for service.

Kempinski Hotel Barbaros Bay $$$$ *Kızılağaç Koyu, Gerenkuyu Mevkii, Yalıçiftlik, tel: 0252-311 0303, www.kempinski-bodrum.com*. Gorgeous, family-friendly resort includes the sumptuous Six Senses spa, several excellent restaurants and water sports, set on a virtually private bay north of Bodrum. 173 rooms, suites and villas.

Lavanta Hotel $$$$ *Yalıkavak, tel: 0252-385 2167, www.lavanta. com.* Crowded Bodrum is 16km away from this garden-set retreat overlooking *Yalıkavak* bay. Wood-floored units all have terraces and some antique furnishings; home-cooked meals are served in a lovely dining room or by the large pool. 8 rooms and 7 remote, self-catering 'residences' also let by the week. Open May 15–Oct 15.

DALYAN

Dalyan Resort $$$–$$$$ *Kaunos Sok. 50, Maraş Mahallesi, tel: 0252-284 5499, www.dalyanresort.com.* Riverside complex that's the town's most comfortable digs, with four grades of tasteful, travertine-tiled units, an airy domed restaurant, rental canoes and a hamam offering mud therapy. Popular with package operators.

Kilim $ *Kaunos Sokağı 11, tel: 0252-284 2253, www.kilimhotel. com.* Attractive and friendly little hotel with good-sized rooms (some air conditioned), proper stall-showers, a palm-shaded pool and indeed plenty of kilims. Riverside annexe where breakfast is served, home-cooked meals (plus regular barbecue nights).

MARMARIS

Dionysos $$$$ *Kumlubük, Bozburun Peninsula tel: 0252-476 7957, www.dionysoshotel.net.* Olive-grove estate hotel with 27 se-cluded villas, some with private pools (complementing the com-munal infinity pool and spa). The restaurant may have delicacies like carpaccio-ed *akya* fish and marinated *orkinos* (tuna), as well as creative desserts. Most units available only through Exclusive Es-capes *(see page 116)*.

LYCIAN COAST

ÇIRALI

Odile $$ *Just north of mid-beach, tel: 0242-825-7163, www.hotel odile.com.* The best-value top-end hotel here comprises 36 large, decently equipped rooms and suites, set in lush gardens around a large pool; there are also private beach loungers. On-site restaurant, mixed clientele and yoga/massage teaching area. Closed Nov–Feb.

FETHIYE

Villa Daffodil $$ *Fevzi Çakmak Caddesi 115, İkinci Karagözler, tel: 0252-614 9595, www.villadaffodil.com.* Mid-range hotel on a landscaped shoreline 1km (0.62 miles) from the centre. A pool, restaurant, hamam and fair-sized rooms, make booking recommended.

KALKAN

Lizo $ *Milli Egemenlik Caddesi, Kalamar Yolu 57, tel: 0242-844 3381, http://lizohotel.com.* Two-wing, family-run hotel near the top of Kalkan, with bar-restaurant, garden and small pool. Great views, exceptionally friendly service and excellent food make this a firm favourite, in spite of the steep walk back from the beach.

Villa Mahal $$$$ *1.5km east of town, easterly bay shore, tel: 0242-844 3268, www.villamahal.com.* At Kalkan's most exclusive lodging, a segmented veranda snakes around 10 irregularly-shaped standard rooms, while steps descend past an infinity pool to the sea and lido – with jaw dropping views en route. A pool suite and two cottages share the same designer-minimalist decor. Open May–Oct.

KAŞ

Deniz Feneri Lighthouse $$$$ *North leg of loop road, 8km out on Çukurbağ Peninsula, tel: 0242-836 2741, UK bookings only via Exclusive Escapes (see page 116).* Luxury hotel with just 12 minimalist doubles or family suites, overlooking gardens tumbling down to a 150m (492 ft) lido and a good (expensive) waterside restaurant. At reception level there's an infinity pool, hamam and area for (excellent) breakfasts. Sunset views over the open sea.

Gardenia $$$ *Hükümet Caddesi 47, Küçükçakıl, tel: 0242-836 1618, www.gardeniahotel-kas.com.* Ambitious boutique hotel with just 11 varied rooms and suites featuring Philippe Starck decor and marble floors distributed over four floors. Buffet breakfast to 11am; no children under 12. Open Apr–Nov.

Hideaway $$ *Eski Kilise Arkası 7 , tel: 0242-836 1887, www.hotel hideaway.com.* Recently refurbished, this is the most attractive budget hotel in town, with airy third-floor rooms and a pricier jacuzzi suite. Features a small plunge pool, a library-lounge, and a stunning rooftop restaurant with homestyle cooking. Open all year.

ÖLÜDENIZ

Montana Pine Resort $$$$ *Ovacık Mahallesi, Hisarönü, tel: 0252-616 7108, www.montanapine.com.* Set on a forested hillside overlooking Ölüdeniz, this self-contained resort has rooms and suites scattered in clusters, two pools, unusually good on-site restaurants, and all other facilities you'd expect in a four-star outfit.

Oyster Residences $$$$ *Middle of Belceğiz promenade, tel: 0252-616 0765, www.oysterresidences.com.* The area's first boutique hotel, so successful it expanded in 2007. The 26 large, wooden-floored rooms with quality soft furnishings surround a fair-sized pool with wooden decking, but they also have direct beach access.

PATARA (GELEMİŞ)

Patara Viewpoint $ *Top of east ridge road, Gelemiş, tel: 0242-843 5184 or 0533-350 0347, www.pataraviewpoint.com.* This long-established hotel has an unbeatable setting, American-style wall showers in the bathrooms, a pool-bar where breakfast is served, and a cushioned, Turkish-style nocturnal terrace with fireplace. Advantageous weekly rates; open March–Nov.

MEDITERRANEAN COAST

ALANYA

Kaptan $$$ *İskele Caddesi 70, tel: 0242-513 4900, www.kaptan hotels.com.* A well-established central hotel near the Red Tower, this makes a great (and affordable) base for exploration. Pool, terrace, bar and two restaurants, one harbour view.

ANTALYA

Hillside Su $$$$ *Konyaalti, 1.5km from centre, tel: 0242-249 0700, www.hillsidesu.com.* Antalya's flashest in-town digs is a dazzlingly cool sea of white with stylish mirror accents. There is a sumptuous spa, private pebble beach, fine dining and a popular bar with nightly entertainment.

Mediterra Art $$ *Zafer Sokağı 5, Kaleiçi, Antalya, tel: 0242-244 8624, www.mediterraarthotel.com.* Comprises three knocked-together Ottoman houses containing a total of 21 rooms and suites furnished with polished wood, exposed stone pointing and carpets. Features a courtyard pool, indoor/outdoor restaurants and bar.

Villa Perla $ *Barbaros Mahallesi, Hesapçı Sokak 26, Kaleiçi, tel: 0242-248 9793, www.villaperla.com.* Beautifully restored, 11-room family-run Ottoman mansion-hotel with a shady courtyard pool and excellent restaurant serving fine vegetarian food.

BELEK

Ela Quality Resort $$$$ *İskele Mevkii, Belek, tel: 0242-710 2200, www.elaresort.com.* Very glamorous and cosmopolitan, this is among the newest of Belek's 5-star resorts catering to golfers, with a private beach, plenty of other sports facilities and evening entertainment for between rounds.

SIDE

Beach House $ *Barbaros Caddesi, tel: 242-753 1607, www.beach house-hotel.com.* Small, friendly hotel with balconied rooms overlooking Side's eastern beach. The resort's first (1965) lodgings, it has plenty of character but is also well managed by an Australian-Turkish couple; affiliated restaurant is run by their son.